KIRBY McCOOK
and the
JESUS CHRONICLES

KIRBY McCOOK

AND THE
JESUS CHRONICLES

STEVE ARTERBURN AND **M. N. BROTHERTON**

ILLUSTRATED BY **DAMIAN ZAIN**

TYNDALE HOUSE PUBLISHERS, INC.
CAROL STREAM, ILLINOIS

Visit Tyndale's website for kids at www.tyndale.com/kids.

TYNDALE is a registered trademark of Tyndale House Publishers, Inc.

Kirby McCook and the Jesus Chronicles: A 12-Year-Old's Take on the Totally Unboring, Slightly Weird Stuff in the Bible, Including Fish Guts, Wrestling Moves, and Stinky Feet

Copyright © 2019 by Marcus Brotherton and Stephen Arterburn. All rights reserved.

Illustrations by Damian Zain. All rights reserved. Tyndale House Publishers, Inc.

Author photograph of Steve Arterburn by Josh Durias Photography, copyright © 2010. All rights reserved.

Author photograph of M. N. Brotherton by Victor Photography, copyright © 2012. All rights reserved.

Designed by Mark Anthony Lane II

Edited by Sarah Rubio

Published in association with the literary agency of WordServe Literary Group, www.wordserveliterary.com

Unless otherwise indicated, all Scripture quotations are taken from the *Holy Bible*, New Living Translation, copyright © 1996, 2004, 2015 by Tyndale House Foundation. Used by permission of Tyndale House Publishers, Inc., Carol Stream, Illinois 60188. All rights reserved.

Scripture quotations marked NIV are taken from the Holy Bible, *New International Version*,® NIV.® Copyright © 1973, 1978, 1984, 2011 by Biblica, Inc.® Used by permission. All rights reserved worldwide.

For manufacturing information regarding this product, please call 1-800-323-9400.

For information about special discounts for bulk purchases, please contact Tyndale House Publishers at csresponse@tyndale.com, or call 1-800-323-9400.

Library of Congress Cataloging-in-Publication Data

Names: Arterburn, Stephen, date- author.

Title: Kirby McCook and the Jesus chronicles / Stephen Arterburn and Marcus Brotherton.

Description: Carol Stream, Illinois : Tyndale House Publishers, Inc., 2019.

Identifiers: LCCN 2018037389 | ISBN 9781496429773 (hc)

Subjects: LCSH: Jesus Christ—Biography—Juvenile literature. | Bible stories, English.

Classification: LCC BT302 .A78 2019 | DDC 232.9—dc23 LC record available at https://lccn.loc.gov/2018037389

Printed in China

25	24	23	22	21	20	19
7	6	5	4	3	2	1

*Not to us, O L**ORD**, not to us, but to your name goes all the glory.*

PSALM 115:1

ACKNOWLEDGMENTS

Hey, that's me! ←

I, Kirby, age 12, would like to thank all the moms and dads and others out there who buy this book—and all the kids who read it.

Thank you, television and video games, for turning our brains into mush and for reminding kids everywhere that books are WAY BETTER because they're like movies *in our minds*.

Thanks to Grandpa McCook and his library full of books from seriously brainy scholars, including Dr. Walter Kaiser, who wrote *The Messiah in the Old Testament*; Dr. Edmund Clowney, who wrote *The Unfolding Mystery: Discovering Christ in the Old Testament*; Dr. Robert Thomas and Dr. Stanley Gundry, who put together *A Harmony of the Gospels*; Dr. John Walvoord and Dr. Roy Zuck, who wrote *The Bible Knowledge Commentary*; Dr. Craig Keener, who wrote *The IVP Bible Background Commentary: New Testament*; and lots more smart dudes.

It's been swell, Linda Howard and publishing team at Tyndale; thanks for taking a chance on a fun-loving kid.

Thank you to a guy with a lot of letters after his name, theological editor Matt Rogers, PhD, MDiv, MA, BA. And to our ultracool early readers Addy, Zach, Amie, D. L. Brotherton, and H. C. Jones. Special thanks to Solomon Arterburn, who suggested that a book like this would help others like him have fun learning about Truth.

To agent Greg Johnson at WordServe Literary—thanks for your awesomeness.

Thank you, friends and family. You really know how to dance.

Thank you, Professor Waffles and Professor Bacon, for inventing the world's most delicious foods.

CONTENTS

A NOTE TO PARENTS AND TEACHERS

You'll notice a lot about Jesus in the pages to come, even as we go through some Old Testament stories. That's because this book is more than a simple retelling of the usual kid-friendly Bible stories.

It's a book that traces Jesus' involvement through the whole larger Story.

We want kids to see Jesus as the main character of the entire Bible, and we want kids to watch Jesus walk through history right from the beginning.

It's important to note that we're not primarily trying to teach morality with this book. We want to inspire kids to draw close to Jesus, to have a relationship with Jesus, and to live in light of God's holiness, sovereignty, and grace.

Here's how this Bible storybook can help:

It's comprehensive. This book looks at the life of Jesus from cover to cover, specifically helping readers see that Jesus has had an important place in God's plan for redemption from the beginning of time.

It's kid friendly and conversational in tone. This book is meant to be enjoyed by kids.

It's fun and lively, humorous but never irreverent. It meets kids on their level, speaking their language and inviting great conversations.

It's biblically and theologically whole. This book takes the whole canon of Scripture into consideration. For instance, when we tell the story of Creation, we also weave in corresponding portions of John 1, Colossians 1, Hebrews 1, and other sections of the New Testament.

It roots and establishes a child in Jesus Christ. We want children to begin to see and think of themselves as *in Christ*. Think of this as an exhorting, identity-establishing book for children in the spirit of Colossians 2:6-7: "Just as you accepted Christ Jesus as your Lord, you must continue to follow him. Let your roots grow down into him, and let your lives be built on him."

It represents a full picture of the character of God. In communicating the gospel of Jesus Christ and the Story of grace, we emphasize God's love, holiness, and sovereignty. All three characteristics of God are important.

We pray that children and families everywhere would follow Jesus, that their lives would be transformed by him, and that ultimately they would join Jesus on his mission. Life is far too short to spend it in rebellion or willful disobedience against God.

Ultimately, we pray that our readers would grow in the grace and knowledge of God. We want them to understand the bigger picture of Jesus, and we pray they would walk closely with Jesus throughout their whole lives. Amen.

> I could have no greater joy than to hear that my children are following the truth.
>
> 3 JOHN 1:4

START READING HERE

Jimmy let out a sneeze louder than a motorbike with no muffler.

And we knew we were doomed.

We were sitting around in junior church that morning while the grown-ups were upstairs in big-people church. All twelve of us kids: Jimmy. Noah. Emma. Olivia. Mason. Felipe. Jayden. My sister Aggy. Aisha. Zuri-Claire. My brother Jo-Jo. And me, Kirby McCook.

The sneeze blasted out of Jimmy's nose. Ka-blaz-a-blam! His sneeze-goop slammed onto the carpet—wham!—and sat there like a pile of steaming monkey barf.

That's when our teacher, Mrs. Higgins, threw up her hands and said, "Oh! I can't do this anymore!"—and walked out.

Jimmy wiped his nose on his shirtsleeve, elbowed Jayden in the guts, and said, "Go see where she's going." So Jayden slunk out to follow Mrs. Higgins from a distance, and that's the last we saw of him for a good eleven minutes till he came back and said, "Guys—she's gone."

"Gone?" Jimmy said. "What do you mean?"

← Yep! That's Jimmy.

1

"Slammed-her-car-door-and-roared-down-the-road gone," Jayden said. "I saw Kirby's Grandpa McCook talking to her before she left, but she still left. I don't think she's coming back. Remember what Mrs. Higgins told us last time Jimmy treated us to a blasto sneeze?"

Aisha sighed. "Mrs. Higgins said her blood pressure went up. 'Way, way, way, way, WAY up.' Whatever that means."

"That's five whole 'ways,'" Jayden said knowingly. "It means we don't have a teacher anymore. We're sunk."

Trembling, Mason said, "Oh no. If we don't have a regular teacher, we'll get Mr. Cowburn as a substitute again. He'll bore us to death!"

Everyone started talking at once, really freaking out.

"HERE'S THE PLAN," Jayden said. He has a real big voice, like his dad, the pastor, so we all got quiet and looked at him. "One of us kids hasta teach junior church today. And the rest of us better listen, because our parents will ask what we learned. Maybe Mrs. Higgins w   ill come back next week."

"So who's going to teach?" said Felipe.

Fifteen silent seconds passed. Then every eyeball looked at me, Kirby McCook, age 12.

Jimmy   Felipe   Emma   Mason   Olivia   Noah

"You do it, Kirbs," Jo-Jo said. "You've been in church forever. You should know something by now."

I looked him square in the eye and said, "Nuts to you, potato-boy, I'm not teaching anything."

"But you have to," Zuri-Claire said. "You're THE BEST." And she gave me a little grin.

"OKAY, I'LL DO IT," I said quickly. Way, way, WAY too quickly. (I have a secret crush on Zuri-Claire. If you tell anyone, I'll punch you in the nose.)

Before my face went ketchup-colored, I walked to the front, and with as much coolness as you ever saw, I said, "Okay, class, what shall we study?"

"Dinosaurs!" Jimmy shouted.

"Not again!" yelled everybody. Jimmy always wanted dinosaurs.

I said, "I'll tell you what we're going to study—Jesus."

"JESUS?" everybody said, like that was such a surprising topic for junior church.

How could I go wrong with that subject? Right?

Aisha   Jayden   Aggy   Jo-Jo   Kirby   Zuri-Claire

1.
JESUS—RIGHT FROM THE START

Ahem.

Everybody listening? Jimmy? Olivia?

Okay. We'll learn about Jesus right from the start. The story of Jesus doesn't start with a baby in a manger. Nope. Not with a shining star hung over a stable, not with shepherds watching sheep sleep. And it certainly doesn't start with three wise guys and their gold, Frankenstein, and myrrh.

Every kid thinks Jesus' story starts at Christmastime, because we like Christmas presents. *Yahoo!*

But Jesus' story actually starts before the beginning of time. Long before there were books or bathtubs or skateboards or purple shag carpets. Long before cheeseburgers or pizza or cookies with sprinkles. Long before anything ever was, Jesus was.

Jesus existed before anything was created. In the beginning was Jesus, and Jesus was with God, and Jesus was God.

Now we all gotta get really brainy here—even Jimmy the Astonishing Sneeze Machine—because usually we just say that God was there before anything else, and when we say "God," we're thinking about God the Father.

But here's this mysterious idea to wrestle with—God in Three Persons, aka the Trinity.

My Grandpa McCook once told me that there's God the Father, God the Son, and God the Holy Spirit, and all three were there as the Great One before anything else existed. That means Jesus' story starts way back when, because Jesus is God the Son. Well, Jesus' story actually has NO START, because he's eternal, which means any start point you can name, Jesus was there before that.

We don't know exactly what God's Son did back then, but he didn't just hang out in heaven, killing time until he wrapped himself in a human body and came to earth as a baby. Nope.

The Bible says that Jesus is "supreme over all creation," and that God created everything through Jesus. Jesus made the things we can see and the things we can't see. Hey, just because you can't see something doesn't mean it doesn't exist.

Think about it: we can't see gravity, but it's real. Throw an apple up and stand directly underneath it. You'll know gravity is real when that apple lands on your head. *Thu-thunk!* Gravity is something Jesus created.

We can't see air, or love, or hate, or radio waves, or subatomic particles like those whatchamacallits— quarks. Thanks for shouting that out, Jimmy. You do use that incredible brain sometimes. Quarks are even tinier than atoms. And all those unseeable things are real.

We can't see God the Father, but he's real. What's one way we know God is real? Because Jesus is the "visible image of the invisible God." Jesus radiates God's glory and expresses God's character.

God the Father had a job for Jesus in the beginning. Jesus gave life and breath to everything. That's right. Jesus was the Designer and Creator. Jesus was the Amazing Person who made this whole universe out of—get this—*nothing*. Yep, his raw material was a big bunch of nothing.

We don't know exactly how Jesus did it. But we know for sure that when the universe came to be, the Father started it all through Jesus.

The bell rang, and we all noticed Grandpa McCook talking to Mr. Javier, the children's minister, outside our classroom window. We all silently left, eyes wide, wondering what would happen next week.

KIRBY'S NOTES

STICK INSIDE YOUR BRAIN

Christ is the visible image of the invisible God. He existed before anything was created and is supreme over all creation, for through him God created everything in the heavenly realms and on earth.

COLOSSIANS 1:15-16

WANNA READ MORE?

John 1:1-3

Acts 17:24

Hebrews 1:2-3, 10

2.
JESUS MAKES DINOSAURS

Well, Grandpa McCook and Mr. Javier both talked to Mrs. Higgins this week. They all decided she was a bit frazzled and needed something called a leave of absence. Sort of like a vacation. Grandpa McCook agreed to take responsibility for our class, but here's the catch. He worked out a plan with Mr. Javier to experiment with team teaching the class with—wait for it—ME.

"Yep," Grandpa told me, "I've always said you kids need to step up and take on some responsibility. Here's your chance, Kirby. You'll be the stand-up guy, and I'll be the resource guy."

And so Grandpa hauled in his beat-up old recliner, dragged the chair to the back of the classroom, and plopped himself in it. "I've got a bum knee," he said, "so here's where you'll find me if you need me." He gave me a wink. "It's all you, buddy."

When he explained all that to the class, I noticed Zuri-Claire beaming at me, and my neck got kind of hot.

Then I stood up front and said, "Okay. Each week I'll tell you a little about whatever I know about Jesus. We won't look at ALL the stories in the Bible—only ones where Jesus shows up. And here's something lots of people don't know—Jesus shows up in WAY MORE stories than you think."

Mason piped up. "I dunno," he said, looking around at the other kids. "There's a lot of hard stuff in the Bible. Kirby's a smart guy, but what if he gets stumped?"

"Don't worry," I said, even though it was probably pointless, because Mason's always worrying about something. "When I get stumped, we'll ask Grandpa McCook. He's been around forever, and he's read the Bible a ZILLION times. He knows Jesus better than anyone else I can think of." From his recliner Grandpa gave a little salute.

Mason smiled for a millisecond, then frowned again. "But we need to keep this under wraps, don't we? Your grandpa's cool, but we can't let most grown-ups know. Otherwise we'll get boring Mr. Cowburn as our substitute FOR SURE!!!!!"

I looked around at the other kids and asked, "Okay, what do you all think?"

Most of the kids nodded in agreement. We all knew this wasn't quite normal for junior church. But it looked like everyone was up for an adventure.

Only one person wasn't smiling. Jimmy folded his arms across his chest, glared, and announced, "It's a dumb idea, Kirby McCook. Your head is filled with oatmeal and sugar donuts. I, for one, don't think you can do it."

That made me jump in with both feet, and I said, "Well, I, for one, think it's a GREAT idea."

Ahem. Uh—your attention please.

Last week we started with when Jesus got started. Er—that is—he never actually started, because he just always was.

Every head swiveled to look at Grandpa, and he nodded and said, "It's called being eternal—no beginning at all. And no ending either." The heads swiveled back to me.

Exactly, just like I said last week. See, Jimmy? We also found out that God the Father, Son, and Holy Spirit teamed up to create everything.

Here's how that went down: at the dawn of time, when God started creating the heavens and the earth, the earth wasn't much to look at. The Bible says it was formless and empty and dark, and it had deep waters covering it. God the Holy Spirit hovered like a helicopter right above those waters. Yep, all three of the God-Persons were active in Creation.

On the first day, God, through Jesus, created light. He just spoke—and light appeared. *Whammo!* And God called the light good.

On the second day, God the Son created the sky. He just spoke—and sky appeared. *Ka-blaza-blam!* And God called the sky good.

The third day, Jesus separated water from land and called the land "earth" and the waters "seas." And that was good. Jesus told the land to produce plants. All kinds of trees and shrubs and vines and blossoms and bulrushes and shoots and leaves and Venus flytraps appeared. And that was all good. Nobody had allergies back then, so nobody was sneezing.

On the fourth day, Jesus created stars, the sun, and the moon. Good, again.

On the fifth day, Jesus created all kinds of living things, first in the seas and next in the air. Sharks and trout and sea horses and clams and oysters. Then eagles and hummingbirds and buzzards and umbrella birds and falcons and cockatiels.

And God called it all good.

On the sixth day, Jesus created all the land creatures. Cows and dogs and hogs and giraffes and snails and dinosaurs (some people think they were called behemoths and leviathans back then). And even slugs. Yeah, slugs. And God called it all good—even slugs.

There must have been lots of noise at first. Imagine all that roaring and bellowing and meowing and whinnying and barking and hee-hawing!

In all that noise and goodness, God the Son created one more important thing on the sixth day—and it was really, really good. Do you know what it was?

Actually, I'm going to leave you guessing.

But remember this: Jesus existed before anything, and God created everything through Jesus.

Okay, see you next week.

KIRBY'S NOTES

STICK INSIDE YOUR BRAIN

In the beginning was the Word, and the Word was with God, and the Word was God.

JOHN 1:1, NIV

WANNA READ MORE?

Genesis 1

Colossians 1:15-20

1 Corinthians 8:6

3.
JESUS JUMP-STARTS HUMANS

Kirby here. Shhhh. I'm talking to YOU and ONLY YOU—you, the reader. Don't tell anyone, okay? Just between you and me, Zuri-Claire doesn't have a phone (not every kid on the planet does), so she wrote me a note. It said,

Your teaching was really interesting last week.

PS Do you like me?

YES ___

NO ___

Hoo boy, what am I ever going to do?! Of course I like her. But I can't tell her—can I?

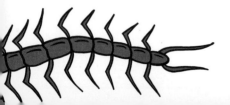

Ahem.

Hey, class, do you know what God created, late on the sixth day of Creation, after he'd done all the animals? God—through Jesus, remember—created one more thing . . .

A dude.

A brand-new human being. But he didn't look like a baby with chubby cheeks and a fat head. He was a full-grown man, and God named him Adam, meaning "human being." Yep, Adam's name was just "man." Like, "Hey, MAN, howzit going?"

At first, Jesus created only one human—and it's important to get this because later we'll see how we were all "in" this one human. We're all chips off the same block, as Grandpa would say, this man that God created in his image.

God called everything he'd created "good." It was good, good, and even more good, and good after that.

No—wait! It was all good, EXCEPT for one thing.

God didn't change his mind or create something *not* good. But something was missing! Until Jesus created a companion for Adam, the man would be alone.

And that wasn't good.

Adam needed to see for himself how alone he was, so God paraded all the animals past Adam to get named. Can you imagine Adam doing this job while God watched and enjoyed the whole show with him?

"Hey, that one with the hundred legs. Let's call that a CENTIPEDE."

"And that animal with the long nose like a vacuum. Let's call that an AARDVARK."

"That one with the big ol' horn on his snout, let's call that a RHINOCEROS."

On it went until all the animals got named. But none of them was the right companion for the man. Not one of the animals could talk to Adam or be his closest friend. Adam was still alone.

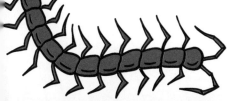

So God put Adam into a deep sleep, took one of his ribs, and made it into another human, a woman named Eve.

God introduced Eve to Adam, who was super excited to meet her. God told Adam and Eve, "Have babies. Fill the earth and rule over it."

God placed the two humans in a perfect environment called the Garden of Eden, where they had everything they needed.

When Adam and Eve got hungry, they could eat right from the Garden. Juicy oranges picked straight off a tree. Grapes and blueberries and strawberries as sweet as candy.

Mmmm. Candy.

Adam and Eve didn't get bored, because they were busy taking care of the Garden. It wasn't backbreaking work that makes you hot and gross and sweaty and tired. Nope, no thorns or thistles in the ground to worry about. God gave Adam and Eve refreshing work—the kind that's so much fun you forget it's work. The kind of work that's meaningful and makes you feel good at the end of the day.

For entertainment, Adam and Eve probably watched the animals. Did you ever see a monkey swing through the trees? Maybe Adam and Eve jumped on an antelope's back and raced across the meadow. They probably laughed to see puppies yip-yap and tumble.

Best of all, each evening in the cool of the day, God came and took a walk in the Garden with Adam and Eve. And as they walked, God listened and talked with the two humans he'd created.

And everything was really, really good.

Part of all this goodness was one special ability that God gave Adam and Eve—the ability to make choices. See, God didn't want them to be robots—machines that were programmed to do whatever he wanted. He longed for Adam and Eve to love and trust and obey him freely because they chose to.

So Jesus planted a tree in the middle of the Garden and told Adam and Eve, "See that tree. DON'T EAT the fruit of that one tree. Not EVER. That's the tree of the knowledge of good and evil, and if you eat that tree's fruit, you'll be disobeying. If you eat that fruit, you'll know evil, and you'll die. You got that, Adam and Eve?"

Adam and Eve both nodded. It wasn't rocket science.

"Good," Jesus said. "Now that we've got that straight, go back to having a wonderful time."

Okay, pop quiz. Question: What was the one thing Adam and Eve were NOT supposed to do?

Well, hama-lama-ding-dong, I knew you were smart!

But will Adam and Eve pass their test? We'll see next week.

KIRBY'S NOTES

STICK INSIDE YOUR BRAIN

There is no fear in love. But perfect love drives out fear. . . . We love because he first loved us.

1 JOHN 4:18-19, NIV

WANNA READ MORE?

Genesis 2–3

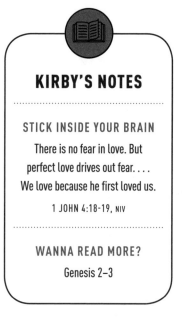

← God doesn't want robots.

4.
JESUS GIVES HOPE TO A SKETCHY WORLD

Still scratching my head over Zuri-Claire's note. If I check yes, she'll think . . . but if I check no, she'll think . . . and if I do nothing . . . thunder turtles! There's no solution!

Oops, time for class to start.

Hi, everybody. You know that perfect environment we talked about, the Garden of Eden? Well, watch out.

One day in the Garden, a fallen angel named Satan slipped and slithered and slunk and slid over in serpent form to the woman, Eve.

The serpent said, "Um, hey, Eve, remember that one thing God told you NOT to do? Question here—did God actually tell you that you can't eat the fruit of any of the trees in the Garden?"

"No," Eve said. "Of course we can eat fruit from the trees

in the Garden. Just not this one right here in the middle. We need to steer clear of that tree. If we eat that fruit or even touch it, then we'll die."

"Uh-uh!" the serpent—sometimes he's also called the devil—said. "Not true. The fruit is good for you. It'll make you wise—just like God. But mean ol' God lied to you, because he doesn't want you to be like him."

See, the sneaky devil always wants us to doubt God, to suspect God's lying to us, which God never does.

Eve edged closer to the tree. She looked at the fruit. She sniffed it. She ran her fingers over the skin. Wow, it was gorgeous. And how could having more wisdom be a bad thing? She began to doubt God.

Eve took a nibble. She chewed and swallowed, and the fruit went down her gullet like a rock. She passed some to Adam, and he ate it too. Then they both realized they were naked. Sheesh, how embarrassing is that! Like that dream when you come to school in only your underwear—but way, way worse. No underwear!

Adam and Eve both disobeyed God, and they both died. They didn't die physically—keel over and stop breathing—right away. That would come later. But that same instant they died spiritually, meaning they were separated from God for the very first time.

This thing called sin—disobedience—came between humans and God and built a great big wall between us. All humans forever were affected when Adam and Eve sinned. Remember that we're all chips off the same block? We all became separated from God. We absolutely can't blast a hole in that wall of sin—it's like it's made of titanium or kryptonite. There's no human machine big enough or superhero strong enough to smash through and get us back with God.

Of course, God's more powerful than any superhero. He can smash the sin wall to reach us—nothing stops him. But sin needs to be dealt with, because God is absolutely holy—awesome, majestic, and mighty—and nothing dirty or polluted like sin can come near him. There's no trace of evil in God, so sin and God just can't be in the same place. But just wait—later we'll see Jesus tear down the wall and deal with our sin.

That evening when Jesus came to walk with Adam and Eve in the cool of the Garden, they hid in the bushes. They were ashamed. They'd never been ashamed before, but sin made them feel shame. They sewed fig leaves around themselves, to try and carry the bushes along and keep hiding.

It didn't work. God knew exactly where Adam and Eve were because he always knows everything. Jesus talked with them about what they'd done. Eve tried to pin all the blame on the serpent, and then Adam blamed Eve. See, *shame*, *blame*, and *hiding* are all part of the ugly stuff of sin. Adam and Eve knew they'd disobeyed God, and now there would be *consequences*.

What does that word mean? It means that if you disobey, then something bad will happen. Maybe something bad will actually happen right away. Or maybe you'll just feel yucky in your heart. You'll know you disobeyed, because you can't cover up that dismal feeling of sin separating you from God. Unless you disobey so much that you get used to that yucky feeling, and you don't even notice it anymore. Then you're in a really big mess, because it's hard for you to tell what's good and what's not.

God never, ever stopped caring for Adam and Eve—just like he never stops caring for you and me. Yet consequences came. God had to throw them out of the Garden of Eden. But God also did something wonderful.

God promised that one day that sin-wall would be blasted away—and the Person who'd do it would be Jesus. One far future day, the serpent would bruise the heel of Jesus' foot, but Jesus would crush the

KIRBY'S NOTES

STICK INSIDE YOUR BRAIN

Jesus spoke to the people once more and said, "I am the light of the world. If you follow me, you won't have to walk in darkness, because you will have the light that leads to life."

JOHN 8:12

WANNA READ MORE?

Galatians 4:4
Hebrews 2:9-10

serpent's head. That means the serpent would hurt Jesus only a little compared to how Jesus would completely trash the devil.

Jesus would TOTALLY WIN!

Just remember: in the midst of the sad, sad story of Adam and Eve disobeying God, Jesus is the ray of light. Ever since then, this world has been pretty messed up—but Jesus is the hope for this fantastic, wonderful, sketchy world.

But before things get better on planet Earth, they'll get worse. We'll find out . . . next week!

5.
JESUS DEALS WITH MESSES

Zuri-Claire's note is driving me crazy. What to do? Between you and me, it's the toughest decision I've ever faced. Oooofff!

Ahem.

We'll start today with explaining a big word: *Christophany.*

You say it *kris-TOFF-an-ee*. And no, it's not the name of your mom's new perfume.

Before class I asked Grandpa McCook about this.

He explained how the Bible says no one has seen God the Father, yet several times God shows up on earth with a body and a voice, and people see and hear him. Lots of brainy scholars believe it's actually Jesus.

God's Son is so near to the Father's heart that Jesus reveals the Father to us. A *Christophany* is when Jesus shows up before his birth. Sometimes Jesus is called "the angel of the Lord." But Jesus is not an angel like Gabriel or those other dudes we sometimes draw with wings. The word *angel* just means "messenger," and Jesus is a Messenger who reveals the Father.

Got that? Good.

Remember when Adam and Eve sinned, sin and death entered the world and spread to everyone. Outside Eden, Adam and Eve found thorns and thistles, and for the first time work became hard. Having babies became hard too.

Adam and Eve had two little boys, Cain and Abel. They grew up and brought offerings to the Lord. Their parents had undoubtedly taught them what kind of offering to bring—only an animal would do, just like blood had been shed and animal skins had covered Adam and Eve's sins in the Garden of Eden. Abel did it right. He was a shepherd, and he brought God the very best lamb from his flock. But Cain was a farmer and brought vegetables. Big yucky zucchini! Wrong move, Cain. You could have traded and brought a lamb to God too. You always need to do what God says. So God didn't accept Cain's offering.

Cain got megamad at his brother—so mad that he killed him. Sin brought about some truly horrible consequences. I mean, sometimes my brother and I argue about stuff, right, Jo-Jo? But to actually kill your own brother— wow, that's really messed up!

Yet even in Cain's extreme disobedience, God still cared for him. If God can care for a rotten dude like Cain, then I guess God can care for anybody. The really good news is that one day, through Jesus, anybody could be forgiven.

Time passed and passed and the Bible tells about a big flood and a guy named Noah who took a wild ride on rough seas with a boatload of animals. That sorta rebooted life on earth.

Centuries went by, and then God zeroed in on one man, Abram, because God planned to use Abram to build a nation and through this nation bring the world a Savior.

I glanced at Grandpa McCook, expecting him to say something like "Right on," but he was quietly snoring. Oh well.

The next place Jesus shows up is in a visit with Abram. Yes, I hear you, Jimmy, insisting the guy's name is *Abraham*, and you're kinda right. The guy's name is changed to Abraham later. But at first, he's just Abram, or Abe for short. Actually, Abe works whether he's Abram or Abraham, so let's just keep it simple and call him that.

God promised Abe and his wife, Sarai, that their descendants would have so many babies they'd be uncountable. See, you need LOTS of babies to create a whole nation.

"That's cool, God," Abe said. "One problem though. Sarai and I don't have A SINGLE SOLITARY KID—and we're getting old. Wrinkly old. Too old to have kids. How do we get uncountable descendants without any kids?"

"Don't worry about that," God said. "You're going to have a son of your own. Look up at the sky and see if you can count all those stars I made. No? Didn't think so. Well, that's how many descendants you're going to have—so many you can't count them."

This was an exciting promise, but it took a long time for Abe and Sarai to see it start coming true. So long that Sarai got fed up with God's plan and figured she and Abe would help God out. She had an Egyptian maid named Hagar, and Sarai said to Abe, "Hey, sweetie-pie husband, instead of you and *me* being the daddy and mommy of our baby, why don't you and *Hagar* be the daddy and mommy?"

Abe said, "Sugar-lips, that's a peachy idea." Then his eyeballs exploded.

Okay, Abe's eyeballs didn't actually explode, but he plowed ahead with a bad plan! DAN-GER! Sirens! Lights! Dogcatcher! Okay, so this sounds like a super crazy idea to us, but in those times it was actually a thing husbands and wives did when they couldn't have kids of their own. But it was NOT what God wanted. God wanted Abram and *Sarai* to be the parents of their baby. Not Abram and *Hagar*. God wanted them to wait for his timing. But nope. They got itchy and impatient and couldn't sit still to wait for God to bring them a baby.

Hagar became pregnant, then Sarai got jealous and mistreated her, so Hagar ditched town. She ran into the wilderness—and Jesus found her beside a spring of water. Hagar said, "You are the God who sees me." It was amazing to her that Abram's God cared about her, even though she was just a servant and had grown up worshiping other gods. Jesus sent her home, because God had a plan for her, too.

Hagar had a healthy baby boy. Abram named him Ishmael. Nothing wrong with the baby himself—he was just a cute, cuddly diaper-filler. It was what Abe and Sarai had *done* that was a big no-no. They didn't stick to each other as husband and wife. They didn't wait for God's timing or follow his instructions.

But here's good news: although Abe and Sarai messed up, God still blessed them. Not for doing wrong, but because he loved them. That's this crazy-wonderful idea of *grace*: God loves us even when we mess up.

Soon after that, God changed Abram's name to Abraham, meaning "father of many," and he changed Sarai, "princess," to Sarah, "princess of many." It was another hint that God would work out his plan to give them all those kids he'd promised. They just needed to believe God.

KIRBY'S NOTES

STICK INSIDE YOUR BRAIN

The Son radiates God's own glory and expresses the very character of God, and he sustains everything by the mighty power of his command.

HEBREWS 1:3

WANNA READ MORE?

John 1:18, 6:46
Romans 5:17
Genesis 12:1-3

6.
JESUS IN DISGUISE

I've got a brainy idea for what to do about Zuri-Claire's note. I'll let you know if it works.

Good morning, class.

(I'm hoping that sounds sort of grown up.)

Did I tell you Abram was an amazing 86 years old when Ishmael was born? But hold onto your socks, more amazing stuff is coming. Thirteen quick years passed. When Abram was 99, God repeated that Abram would become the father of many descendants, and *Sarai would be the mother*. That was God's plan in the first place, if they'd just waited. They were supposed to believe what God said—that's called faith. Remember that God changed their names to Abraham and Sarah.

Here's where Jesus enters Abraham's story again. One day three men came and had

Fire and brimstone . . . meet Earth.

24

supper with Abraham. (*Psst*—it was actually one of those Christophanies—Jesus and two angels in disguise.) While they were having dinner, Jesus told Abraham to circle the calendar date—Sarah's baby would come in one year's time. Sarah was sitting inside her tent, listening in to the conversation. When she heard this, she laughed and laughed and then laughed some more. *Bah-ha-ha!* Sarah was 89 years old at this point—WAY too old to have a baby. She couldn't swallow this.

Bad move, Sarah. She messed up first when she got tired of waiting for God's perfect plan and took matters into her own hands. Now she was messing up again by not believing that God could do a miracle and bless her with a baby. She forgot that God is always good, he always loves us, and nothing is too hard for him.

Meanwhile, Abraham's nephew, Lot, lived in a rotten city called Sodom. This city was ugly and stinky and super wicked. Jesus told Abraham that God was going to destroy the city, but Abraham didn't want the city wiped out, probably because he cared about his nephew, so Abraham negotiated with Jesus, asking, "What if the city has fifty righteous people—will you still destroy it?"

"Nope," Jesus said. "If I find fifty righteous people there, I'll spare the city."

"How about forty-five righteous people?"

"Nope. It'll still be spared."

"Um . . . forty?"

"Nope."

"Uh, how about . . ."

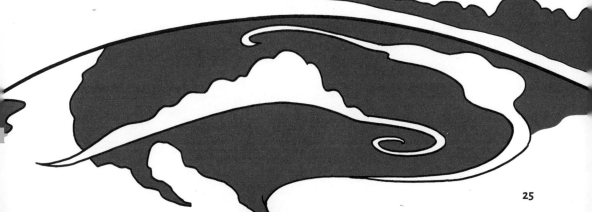

And so on and so on, until Abraham got down to just ten—and Jesus agreed. But not even ten righteous people were found in Sodom, so God rained down fire from the sky and destroyed the city. Fortunately, Lot and his family got out of the city in the nick of time. Unfortunately, Lot's wife looked back, maybe because she liked that city so much, and she was turned into a salt statue.

It's kind of a crazy story with all these negotiations going on beforehand, and then God blasting the city—so I asked Grandpa McCook about it. He said it's a tricky story. Basically, all nations were going to be blessed through Abraham, but because of God's justice, one humongously evil city needed to be removed first. By allowing Abraham to negotiate with him, God was inviting Abraham to work with him. God was inviting Abraham to pray some big prayers on behalf of lost people who did not love God.

Remember all that laughing about Sarah getting pregnant? Exactly one year later, Abraham and Sarah had a beautiful healthy boy. A miracle baby. They named him "Isaac," which means—wait for it—"he laughs."

After all the happy diapers and bottles and goo-goo-ing and baby rattles, something sad happened. Ishmael, who was a teenager now, teased Isaac something fierce, even bullying him, so Ishmael and Hagar were sent away. They wandered in the wilderness and nearly died of thirst.

But God called to Hagar and said, "Don't worry, I'm going to make your son a great nation too." God opened Hagar's eyes, and she saw a well full of water. And both Hagar and Ishmael were saved.

Abraham felt pretty good after Isaac was born. He had the son that God had promised. All was well. But after the blessing came a test. A super hard test.

KIRBY'S NOTES

STICK INSIDE YOUR BRAIN

Trust in the LORD with all your heart and lean not on your own understanding; in all your ways submit to him, and he will make your paths straight.

PROVERBS 3:5-6, NIV

WANNA READ MORE?

Hebrews 1:1-3
Genesis 18:25
Hebrews 11:8-12

In fact, it was the test of all tests. God said to Abraham, "Take your son and sacrifice him to me as a burnt offering."

Abraham gulped. "You mean Isaac?"

Yep. Isaac.

So Abraham and Isaac hiked up Mount Moriah. Abraham built an altar, tied up his son, and placed him on the altar. Isaac was like, "What's happening, Dad?" Abraham took out a knife and prepared to sacrifice his son. And that's where we'll stop the story for now. Right there. With the knife raised over Isaac's head.

(Cue scary shark-movie music: duuun dun, duuun dun, dun dun dun dun dun dun dun.)

7.
JESUS
RULES

Shhhh—you and me are buds, right? So keep this to yourself, PLEASE! I put an X on Zuri-Claire's note, and I gave it to Emma, who gave it to Olivia, who gave it to Aggy, who gave it to Aisha, who gave it back to Zuri-Claire.

Where did I put the X? Well, I wrote another word on the note—MAYBE—and I checked that box. I'm so smart.

I hope that works. But I dunno. Zuri-Claire just read the note right now and looked kind of confused.

Okay, gotta teach!

Ahem.

We left off with a cliff-hanger. Remember? I know you're desperate to see how the story ends, and I should hurry up, but since today's story starts with Isaac, and Isaac's name means "laughter," I'd say it's a good time for a joke.

What do you call a rabbit that lives under your bed?

Give up?

A dust bunny. Ha ha ha ha . . .

Are you guys awake? Come on, that was a good one! Okay, okay, on with the story.

This part really isn't funny. Just as the knife was coming down, Jesus called to Abraham from heaven. "Stop! Don't harm your son! Now I know that you love and trust God. You won't hold anything back." Abraham believed God could actually raise his son back to life if Abraham went through with the killing, because God had promised Isaac would become a father.

Well, Abraham passed the test. A ram was stuck by its horns in a thicket, and God told Abraham to sacrifice the ram instead. Jesus said, "Because you've obeyed God, you'll be blessed. God will multiply your descendants beyond number, like stars in the sky and sand on the seashore. Through your descendants all the nations of the earth will be blessed."

Isaac grew up and got married to a woman named Rebekah. Isaac and Rebekah had twin sons, Esau and Jacob. Esau liked to play outdoors, growing up hunting, trapping, yelling, and shouting. Esau was Isaac's favorite. But Rebekah loved Jacob most. Jacob liked to play indoors. He was a quieter kid, and that's okay. Quieter kids have fun too.

One day Esau was out hunting. He didn't catch anything, and he came home crazy starving. Jacob, hanging around the home tents like usual, had just cooked supper.

"STEW!" Esau said. "MUST. EAT. NOW."

"Not so fast," Jacob said. "It'll cost you."

"HOW MUCH?"

"Your birthright."

29

Okay, now I gotta explain about birthright. Although they were twins, Esau had been born first, slightly before his brother. In those days, when a father died, everything he owned would be passed along to his kids. A birthright was a double share of the inheritance loot. The oldest son got twice as much as the younger ones, and the oldest son also became the head of the family. Birthright meant honor and possessions and spiritual leadership. Real value.

"What good is a birthright if I die of hunger?" Esau yelled. "Quick—GIMME SOME STEW!"

Jacob sold him the stew, and that wasn't cool of Jacob. Jacob charged way, way too much for a measly bowl of stew. Esau did wrong too. Esau didn't value his birthright. He sold it way, way too cheap.

Time passed, and Isaac, their dad, grew really old and blind and was expected to die soon, so he called his firstborn into his tent and said, "Esau, get your bow and arrows and hunt me some of that tasty wild game I love so much. Come home and roast it up, and then I'll eat it and bless you."

Esau went off hunting. But Rebekah had overheard the conversation, and she wanted Jacob to get the blessing instead, so she hatched a scheme. "Hey, Jacob," she said. "Go to the backyard and get two young goats from our flock. I'll cook a quick dinner just the way your father likes it. You give your dad the food, and then he'll bless you before Esau gets back."

"But Esau's a hairy dude," Jacob said. "What if Dad touches my arms? He'll know I'm lying."

"Wear your brother's stinky hunting clothes," Rebekah said. "And cover your hands and neck with goatskins. Dad will never know the difference."

Bad news!!! That's lying. Stealing. Impersonating a stinky hunter. WRONG! Jacob did everything his mom told him to do. Normally that's good, but this time, it was not. Jacob went into Isaac's tent and said, "Here you go, Dad. Eat up and bless me."

"Wow, that was really quick hunting," Isaac said. "Come here so I can touch you.

Huh. You feel like Esau, but you sound like Jacob—what's the deal?"

"Uh, I dunno, I'm definitely Esau," Jacob said.

Isaac ate the food Jacob had brought, then he beckoned him closer. When Jacob kissed his dad, Isaac smelled Esau's clothes and said, "I guess it really is Esau."

So Isaac blessed Jacob. He blessed him and blessed him and blessed him.

Later, Esau came in from his hunting trip and learned he'd been tricked again. He was super mega-angry. So angry, in fact, that he vowed to kill his brother. Rebekah told Jacob to run for his life. Not much else he could do now. NOT following Grandpa Abraham's example of trusting and obeying God, both Esau and Jacob landed in big trouble.

KIRBY'S NOTES

STICK INSIDE YOUR BRAIN

Give me understanding, so that I may keep your law and obey it with all my heart. Direct me in the path of your commands, for there I find delight.

PSALM 119:34-35, NIV

WANNA READ MORE?

Genesis 22:1-18
Hebrews 11:17-19
Genesis 25:27-34

8.
JESUS—CHAMPION WRESTLER

Zuri-Claire is acting really cool. And I don't mean COOL cool. I mean cold as ice. She won't even look at me. What did I do wrong?

Ahem. Hi, everybody.

Well, Jacob ran far away to the home of Laban, his mom's brother. Laban had two daughters, Leah and Rachel, and soon Jacob fell in love with Rachel. Jacob said to Uncle Laban, "I really want to marry your daughter Rachel. How about I work for you for free for seven years if you'll give her to me as my wife?"

Laban's eyes gleamed, and he said, "That sounds great to me. In seven years she's all yours."

"Good deal," said Jacob, and off he went to work. He worked and worked and worked. He was so in love with Rachel that the years just flew by.

Seven years later Jacob married Rachel . . . or so he thought. Back then a woman wore lots of wedding veils and stuff, so it was hard to see her face. The morning after the wedding, Jacob woke up happy. "Morning, Rachel, sweetie-pie, lovie-bird, ready for breakfast?" He rolled over and looked at his wife.

BUH-NUH-NUH-NUH-NUH?!?!?

It wasn't Rachel at all! It was Leah. Jacob had married the wrong woman! Jacob didn't love Leah. He loved Rachel. Every moment of every day for seven years, he'd dreamed of marrying Rachel!

Jacob ran to Laban. "You tricked me! What gives?!"

Laban hemmed and hawed. "Well, somebody had to marry Leah. In our customs, the older daughter always gets married first. Look—here's a bright idea: marry them both. You can marry Rachel next week, then work for me another seven years—free. Everything will be fair and square."

Jacob was up a creek. "Fine!" he said. He waited a week, married Rachel, and now had two wives. What a crazy, mixed-up situation.

The two wives fought, always jealous of each other. Pretty soon Leah started having babies. In those days, more kids meant more honor. Leah had four boys—Reuben, Simeon, Levi, Judah—boom, boom, boom, boom. Rachel wasn't getting pregnant, which drove her totally crazy. So Rachel gave her maid to Jacob as a servant-wife, because in that ancient culture any children born to the maid were considered Rachel's. Rachel's maid had two sons, Dan and Naphtali. "Ha!" Rachel said. "I am totally winning the baby war." That just goes to show you how messed up the family had become.

It had been awhile since Leah had gotten pregnant, so she decided to give Jacob her maid too. Leah's maid also had two sons, Gad and Asher. Then Leah had two MORE sons, Issachar and Zebulun. She also had a daughter named Dinah. So at this point Jacob had ten sons and one daughter.

Rachel still really wanted a baby of her own. And finally God gave her one—Joseph—a fine, healthy boy.

Finally, Jacob decided he and his bunch would go home. Jacob made some shrewd business dealings with Laban and got lots of goats and stuff. Laban wasn't happy—no surprise—so Jacob and family fled without saying good-bye. But Laban chased them and caught up with them. He and Jacob talked it out and patched things up, and Jacob and his family went on their merry way.

Then Jacob needed to face another angry man—his brother, Esau—who was riding toward him with an army of 400 men. Jacob was shaking in his boots. He remembered how he'd wronged Esau.

And that's where Jesus enters the story.

The night before Jacob met Esau, Jesus came to Jacob and wrestled with him until sunrise. That's right—God's invisible world touched Jacob's visible world, and Jacob fought with God. It's another one of those Christophanies. Not many details of the fight are recorded, but just imagine a real brawl complete with dropkicks, backbreakers, and brainbusters.

It wasn't because Jesus was weak that the fight lasted so long. Nope. Jesus could have pinned Jacob in a second. But Jesus just let Jacob fight and fight, because that was Jacob's nature—he was a scrapper, always trying to get his way with God. Jesus let him get it out of his system. Jesus didn't finish the fight until the very end, when Jesus threw a blow that wrenched Jacob's hip right out of the socket. *BAM!* Ouch!

Fight over. Jacob finally learned he couldn't beat God.

Duh. The New Testament says Jacob actually "won," meaning he won a blessing from God and an appreciation for God's power. See, when the wrestling match stopped, Jacob asked for a blessing, so Jesus changed Jacob's name.

Jacob means "deceiver"—and Jacob had certainly lived up to that lousy name. But Jesus changed Jacob's name to Israel, meaning "God fights" or "God rules." The course of Jacob's life was changed. Instead of fighting against God, Jacob would now trust God to fight for him. Jacob knew he couldn't rely on his natural strength anymore. He'd have to rely on his God. Israel would also become the name of the nation that God would build to bring the Savior.

More than ever, Jacob needed to rely on God. Because, remember, Jacob had one more tough guy to face—Esau with his 400 soldiers.

We'll find out soon what happened.

Remember: you can fight against God, or trust God to fight for you. Which would you rather do?

KIRBY'S NOTES

. . . .

STICK INSIDE YOUR BRAIN
[Jacob] met God face to face, and God spoke to him—the LORD God of Heaven's Armies, the LORD is his name!

HOSEA 12:4-5

. . . .

WANNA READ MORE?
Genesis 29–32
Hosea 12:3-6

9.
JESUS STOPS A TERRORIST

Zuri-Claire is definitely NOT speaking to me. I said hi this morning, and she sort of lowered her eyebrows. Man, I guess I blew it with that note thing.

Ahem.

All right, dudes. Remember, Jacob was worried about meeting Esau? But they met and hugged it out. The brothers had both grown up a bit over the years. Their shenanigans were over, and they forgave each other. Yay!

Later on something sad happened. Jacob's wife Rachel became pregnant again, and the baby was born okay, but Rachel died. Jacob was totally sad. He named his new baby Benjamin, "son of my right hand." In total, Jacob had twelve sons who would become leaders of twelve important tribes, the framework of the nation God was building.

Years passed, and Jacob's son Joseph went to Egypt and rose to be second-in-command to the king of Egypt, the pharaoh. He protected the whole family there, but that's a story for another time.

Their descendants had lots of babies, and many generations passed. A new pharaoh, who'd never heard of Joseph, came to power in Egypt and did a totally cruel thing. He made all Jacob's descendants become SLAVES, forcing them to make bricks of mud and straw.

For 400 long years the Israelites were slaves. During this time, they came to be called Hebrews. Grandpa McCook told me the word *Hebrews* might mean people "beyond the river," or people who "overcome."

The new pharaoh was like a terrorist who did something even more horrifying than slavery. He wasn't happy with how huge the Hebrew population was getting—he was worried that if there were too many of them they might fight against the Egyptians and take off—so he ordered all newborn Hebrew boys to be thrown into the Nile River. Yep. Girls could live. But baby boys were goners.

During that horrible time, one family with a son, Aaron, and a daughter, Miriam, had a new baby—yep, a baby boy. They hid the kid for three months.

But it got harder and harder. Ever tried to hide a baby? Well, don't. There's the diapers and the crying and the baby food and the—did I say *diapers*? I'm telling ya, IT AIN'T PRETTY.

So they waterproofed a basket, put the baby inside, and placed the basket in the reeds along the Nile's bank. Miriam played along the river-bank so she could watch the basket.

Just then, Pharoah's daughter came to the river to take a bath. There weren't

This Pharaoh guy was the worst.

37

any showers or stuff back then, so the river was probably the best they could do. I can imagine the conversation between her and her attendants:

"Oh, girls, did you bring my favorite shampoo? No, not the stuff made of papyrus—it smells like—WHAT IN THE WORLD IS THAT?!"

Pharaoh's daughter spotted the basket and sent a slave girl after it. Inside was a brand-new PUPPY.

What?

No, not a puppy. Just seeing if you're paying attention. Inside was the crying BABY, and Pharaoh's daughter lifted him and looked him up and down and said, "Oooooh, lookit, a little itty-bitty baby. He's sooooooo cute. He's hungry. Yes, he is. Who's hungry? You are! Yes, you are."

Pharaoh's daughter chose right then and there: THIS BABY WILL LIVE.

Miriam thought quick. She burst from the bulrushes, sprinted up to Pharaoh's daughter, and said, "Hey there, ma'am, want me to get a Hebrew woman to nurse him for you? Babies are a lot of work, you know. Feeding. Burping. Hiccuping. Changing. Chin wiping. Barfing. Nose wiping . . ."

"Yeesh!" Pharaoh's daughter said. "Yes, go! Now!"

Miriam ran, found her mother, and introduced her to Pharaoh's daughter as a baby nurse with excellent references. Pharaoh's daughter said, "Look after this baby for me, and I'll pay you big money!!!" How's that for hilarious? I love this part of the story! That little tyke, whose life was hanging by a thread moments earlier, was back in his mother's arms—and she'd get paid to look after him.

Pharaoh's daughter named the baby Moses, meaning "lifted out" of the water. His biological parents raised him for the next few years, then he lived in the palace and officially became the son of Pharaoh's daughter.

We aren't told exactly what Moses learned during those early years at home with his mom and dad, but I'm pretty sure they told him about God. Probably every chance they got they whispered, "*Pssst.* God loves you. Make sure you don't ever forget about God." They had a hunch Moses would do important work for God, so they taught him good stuff, solid truth, loyalty, and knowledge of right and wrong.

As an older boy and teenager and young man, Moses grew up in the palace. Those were important years too—years of education. I'm sure he learned all the insider information about palace life. Probably how to hold his pinky finger when he ate grapes. How to negotiate with camel train drivers for exotic spices. How to pin an opponent with a dagger. He was trained to be a leader in Egypt.

Moses lived in the palace until age forty. One day, while taking a walk, he saw an Egyptian beating a Hebrew slave. Moses was ticked. This Hebrew was his own countryman. Moses looked this way and that and thought nobody was watching. He jumped the Egyptian, killed him, and hid the body in the sand.

But there were eyewitnesses to the murder, and they told Pharaoh. Moses ran for his life—and out in the outback he met Jesus. Did Moses get away? We'll find out next week.

KIRBY'S NOTES

STICK INSIDE YOUR BRAIN
I am certain that God, who began the good work within you, will continue his work until it is finally finished on the day when Christ Jesus returns.

PHILIPPIANS 1:6

WANNA READ MORE?
Exodus 1:1–2:10
Hebrews 11:23-27
Psalm 121:7-8

10.
JESUS AND
THE BLOODY LAMB

I'll admit it: I'm miserable—and over a GIRL. I can't even figure out how to talk to her, but I saw her and Mason talking and laughing like it was easy as pie. Maybe I should just give up.

Ahem.

After he murdered the Egyptian guy, Moses ran away to the land of Midian, where he met a man named Jethro who had seven daughters. Eventually Moses married one of the daughters, Zipporah, and got a job looking after Jethro's flocks. Big change for Moses—from the palace to the outback. But Moses learned important lessons in those next 40 years working as a shepherd, lessons he'd use later: how to find water, how to move stuff around in the desert, how to be patient and not murder people (he had to use that one a lot).

Let's chart this out. Moses was trained to A) know God; B) understand Egypt; C) live in the desert. Put them together, and what do you get? A dude perfectly suited to lead the Israelites out of slavery. But would he do it?

Here's where Jesus—God the Son—enters the story.

One afternoon out in the desert, Moses saw a bush that was on fire. The bush burned and burned but didn't burn up. Moses went closer to check it out. Then, from inside the burning bush, Jesus' voice called, "Take off your sandals, Moses. You're standing on holy ground."

Moses immediately went barefoot.

Jesus said, "My people are living in miserable slavery. I'm going to rescue them, and you can help. I'll lead them out of Egypt to the Promised Land. They won't be slaves anymore, and everybody will love it. So go tell Pharaoh, 'LET MY PEOPLE GO.'"

Moses was worried because he didn't know God's personal name. How would Moses convince the Israelites to follow if he didn't know the name of the one who told him to lead?

God told Moses an amazing thing: "My name is I AM WHO I AM."

Moses worked his mind around that. God's name means God exists. Period. God has always existed, always will exist, and exists right now. God is ever-present. GOD ALWAYS IS.

But Moses still wasn't ready to get on board with God's plan. "Okay, but I'm not much of a talker, Lord. I've been out with sheep for 40 years. About all I can say anymore is *baaa*."

"I'll be the judge of who can speak and who can't," Jesus said. "After all, I'm the one who made mouths and tongues and all that stuff."

"But I just don't want to, God," Moses whined. "Please send anyone else!"

"Take your big brother, Aaron," Jesus said. "He speaks well. And I'll be with both of you the whole time. Now get a move on."

So Moses and Aaron did exactly what God told them. They walked up to Pharaoh and said, "Look, dude, you can't keep these slaves anymore. God said so. You got to set them free."

"God? Who's God?" Pharaoh said. "I don't know God. I'm Pharaoh, and I'm more powerful than any God."

"You actually think so?" Moses and Aaron said. "Man, you're in for some hard knocks. Just watch."

Then God sent plagues to Egypt—one right after the other. First, the Nile River turned to blood. Then frogs hopped everywhere. Then came swarms of tiny flies called gnats. Then came bigger flies. Then all the farm animals died of plague. Then the Egyptians themselves got sick. Then came hail. Then grasshoppers swarmed in and ate whatever was left of the crops after all that other stuff. Then it was completely dark for three days straight.

It was a bad, bad time to live in Egypt.

Sometimes, after a plague, Pharaoh would say to Moses, "Okay, I guess God really does exist. He's pretty powerful after all. I'll let the Israelites go free. Just take this blasted plague away."

So God took the plague away.

But then Pharaoh would change his mind. "Nope. Fooled you! The Hebrews are still my slaves. Tough darts, buddy."

The very last plague was the most powerful of all. God announced that all the firstborn sons in Egypt would die. The angel of death would travel over the land and kill people, cattle, sheep, donkeys—any person or animal that was the first son in its family.

There was only one way to be safe.

God said to just take the blood of a lamb—a perfect lamb with nothing wrong with it—and sprinkle it on the sides and top of your front door. The angel would see the blood and pass over that house.

Again, Pharaoh didn't listen. So an angel, following God's orders, went up and down every street in every city in Egypt. If the angel saw lamb's blood on the door of a house, he passed over. But if not, then every firstborn son in that house died.

Family after family didn't listen to God. A huge wail rose all over Egypt. People screamed and moaned. Even Pharaoh lost his firstborn son.

Finally, Pharaoh summoned Moses and Aaron and said, "Beat it. Scram. Take all the Israelites and go."

"Yeah, but this time are you for reals?" Moses and Aaron asked.

Pharaoh nodded.

So the Israelites left Egypt at last—free.

Remember the Passover lamb? The lamb who died in the place of others? That's a picture of Jesus, the Lamb of God who takes away the sin of the world. Many years later, Jesus would die on the cross so people could be set free from a far worse slavery— slavery to sin.

Next week, we'll meet some secret SPIES.

KIRBY'S NOTES

STICK INSIDE YOUR BRAIN

God paid a ransom to save you from the empty life you inherited from your ancestors. And it was not paid with mere gold or silver, which lose their value. It was the precious blood of Christ, the sinless, spotless Lamb of God.

1 PETER 1:18-19

WANNA READ MORE?

Acts 7:30-36
Romans 5:8
1 Peter 1:18-19

11.
JESUS THE SUPERSPY

I talked to Aggy about what to do about Zuri-Claire. She said I should write HER a note and explain things. Hmmm. Gotta think about that.

"Let's start with a game of I Spy," I said.

"I'll go first," yelled Mason. "I spy with my little eye something . . . gross." Everybody started laughing.

Jimmy guffawed and pointed. "Kirby's got spinach stuck in his teeth."

"Uh, that's not what I had in mind," I muttered, working my tongue and finger to fix the problem. "Let's skip the game."

Grandpa grinned too, so I tried to be a good sport. I shrugged and grinned myself.

Ahem.

Okay, just pointing out that this is a spy story.

After the Israelites left Egypt, they hiked around the desert, getting sunburned, emptying sand from their shoes, watching spectacular sunsets, and learning to obey God. This is when God gave them the famous Ten Commandments and other good rules. Any self-respecting nation needs a good set of laws, and for this nation God himself gave the law—he even chiseled it onto stone tablets.

Next, the nation needed land—a place to set up shop and grow crops and build houses—and the Promised Land loomed just ahead. They reached the border, where they played a sort of spy game. At God's command, Moses sent twelve spies into the land for forty days to see what was what.

The spies lurked around and spied out stuff and finally reported, "Wow—this land is really cool. Milk. Honey. Cattle. Sheep. Flowers. Vegetables. Space for everyone. Rivers and lakes and good soil for planting. We'd love living in the Promised Land!" The spies brought back delicious fruit, including a single clump of grapes so big it took two men to carry it on poles. Imagine all the grape juice that would make!

All the people cheered: "Y-a-a-a-y."

But the spies added, "There's bad news too, dudes. The land is filled with tough warriors. Lots. Strong. Big. We're like grasshoppers beside them. There ain't no way we can go there. It just can't be done."

All the people booed: "B-o-o-o-o."

Two spies—Joshua and Caleb—didn't agree with the rest. Joshua and Caleb were looking at the land through Superspy Jesus' eyes, and of course Jesus knew all about the big guys but still said to take the land—it was theirs. So Joshua and Caleb were like, "Don't listen to those fraidy cats. God is on our side. The enemy soldiers might be big and strong, but our God is way bigger and way stronger! C'mon, let's go."

But the people wouldn't listen. They shook in their boots with fright. So God said, "Okay. Have it your way. Go trek through the desert for forty years. You'll all die out there, except Joshua and Caleb, because they obeyed me. This whole disobedient generation will

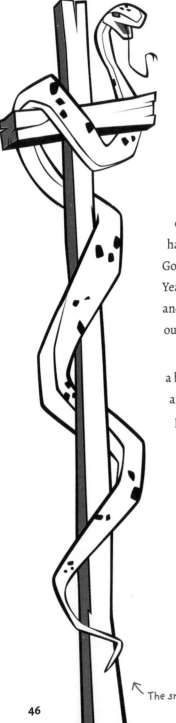

die, and your children can go into the Promised Land instead."

So the Israelites turned away from Canaan, that Promised Land, to go wander in the wilderness again. Well, they didn't exactly *wander*. God was still with them. Even though they hadn't trusted him fully, God led and guided and provided. He snapped his fingers and food appeared on the desert floor. They collected this manna, something like really nutritious cornflakes, every day except Saturday, their day of rest, but they always had enough Friday leftovers for Saturday. Time after time, God performed miracles so they always had water to drink. Year after year they traveled in the burning hot desert sand and grit and gravel, and their shoes and clothes didn't wear out. They always had exactly what they needed.

Once when the people grew impatient and complained, a bunch of snakes slithered out and bit them. Moses prayed, and God told him to make a bronze snake and put it on a pole. People just had to look at the snake, and they'd live. That incident later became a picture of how Jesus works with us. Jesus is lifted up, and anyone who "looks at him" (believes in him) has eternal life.

Finally, everybody in the old generation died except Moses, Joshua, and Caleb. It was time to approach the land again. And this time, they'd do things right.

Moses—really old by then, like 120 years old—stood on the eastern shore of the Jordan River, the border of the Promised Land, and gave the Israelites one final farewell sermon. Moses reviewed all that God had done for them.

The snake is symbolic of Jesus.

He made sure this new generation knew the law. Then he sang them a long, long song.

Then God told Moses, "Go climb a mountain." So he climbed Mount Nebo in the land of Moab, east of the Jordan River. God said, "Look over the river into the Promised Land." God showed him the whole spread. Mega-old Moses couldn't go into the land, because of a time years before when he didn't do what God told him to, but God allowed him to see the land just before he died.

KIRBY'S NOTES

STICK INSIDE YOUR BRAIN

The LORD says, "I will guide you along the best pathway for your life. I will advise you and watch over you."

PSALM 32:8

WANNA READ MORE?

Numbers 13:1–14:9
Psalm 139:23-24

12.
JESUS CARRIES A BIG SWORD

I wish I knew how to write a note to a cute girl without being mushy or making her mad. Google gave me 8,681,329 results. Time to start research.

Ahem.

Joshua, that smart and capable spy, became Israel's new leader. He probably told his generals, "Guys, sharpen your weapons. A bunch of battles are coming, and it won't be easy."

Were they worried?

Probably.

But God told Joshua, "Be strong and courageous! Do not be afraid or discouraged. For the LORD your God is with you wherever you go."

Off to the land where Abraham, Isaac, and Jacob had lived, the land God had promised them, the land called—uh—THE PROMISED LAND. Duh.

The first big job was to cross the Jordan River. There was no shallow spot they could just wade through. The river ran deep and fast. It was flood season. Think rapids, rocks, undertow.

Once across and in the Promised Land, Israel would need to drive out the

Canaanites, people absolutely stuffed full of evil. God would lead Israel smack up to Jericho, one of the toughest, most fortified cities on earth. Jericho had a huge wall around it, one thick enough to build houses on top of. No piece of cake to conquer that.

Why would God let them face such hard stuff? This was a new generation, and if things were easy-peasy, then they'd never learn to trust God. They had to wade into the deep waters and get their feet wet. Then—*whammo!* God would take care of the rest.

God told Joshua, "Here's how you cross the river. I'll lead, and the priests are to carry the Ark into the river. Then have everybody follow. Trust me."

The priests started—

NOT this ark →

Grandpa cleared his throat.

Oh, yeah. The Ark the priests were carrying wasn't Noah's Ark. The word *ark* has another meaning. This was the *Ark of the Covenant*, a special holy box holding three things: stone tablets with the Ten Commandments; Aaron's old staff, which had once miraculously bloomed with flowers; and a gold container filled with manna.

So off they marched: God first, then the priests carrying the Ark, and sure enough, as soon as their feet got wet, the Jordan River parted. A miracle! The water just backed off and piled up in a heap like sand. Then the whole nation walked across the river on dry ground— just like when their parents had crossed the Red Sea.

Then the Israelites walked right up close to Jericho's gates, and here's where Jesus enters the story again. Joshua saw a man standing in front of him with a drawn sword.

"Are you friend or enemy?" Joshua asked.

"I'm the commander of the Lord's Army," Jesus answered.

Joshua fell to the ground and worshiped him. "I'm your servant. What do you want me to do?"

Jesus said, "This city is yours. And here's my wild plan for how you are to take it. Instead of storming the gates, I want you to march around the city for six days, priests leading. Walk around once each day for six days. Don't shout or even say a word. On the seventh day, walk around the city seven times, then the priests are to blast their horns, and I want you to yell. I mean top-of-your-lungs YELL!"

So the people marched and marched for six days, then on the seventh they marched and yelled, and the walls of Jericho crumbled and fell flat. Israel took the city. Job done. Everybody acknowledged that God had won the fight, because no way on earth could people think up such a battle plan.

Only a woman named Rahab and her family in Jericho were spared. Earlier, she'd hidden some Israelite spies and believed God had given the land to Israel. So God honored her.

One by one, key cities in the Promised Land were conquered by Israel. After seven years, they finally had the bulk of the job done.

Then they had a big party, and the leaders divided the land into chunks. Each tribe received a chunk—all except the tribe of Levi, the priests. They were to spread out to all the cities so there'd be priests everywhere.

There was some mopping up to do—a few cities still to conquer. But the wars were basically over, and the Israelites drank a lot of milk and ate a lot of honey and had a grand old time. You'd think this would be a happy ending, but things weren't happy for long.

After a while Joshua and all his generation died, and a new generation grew up in Israel.

They never completely got rid of all the Canaanites. This is important. God's people did MOST of the things God told them to do, but not ALL. And things got really rough for Israel.

Just remember: if there's something difficult in your life, go to God and pray about it. If the difficult thing is something God wants you to do, then with God's help, you can do it, and you can do it ALL the way.

Okay, see you crazy bunch next week.

KIRBY'S NOTES

STICK INSIDE YOUR BRAIN

This is my command—be strong and courageous! Do not be afraid or discouraged. For the LORD your God is with you wherever you go.

JOSHUA 1:9

WANNA READ MORE?

Joshua 1:8-9

Joshua 6

Hebrews 9:1-5

13.
JESUS HAS A CODE NAME

I am definitely going to write Zuri-Claire a note. For sure.

Next week. Yep. Definitely next week.

Ahem.

Ready to rip, potato chip?

After Joshua died, Israel was a big mess, and everybody pretty much just did what they wanted. The Israelites did a bunch of bad stuff and even started worshiping idols.

The Lord put some folks called judges in place to govern Israel. Some judges turned out to be good guys. Others, not so much. When Israel had a good judge and the people followed them, then they did okay. But when Israel had a bad judge, then everything went sideways.

Some judges were sort of good and bad mixed, like Samson. Right before Samson was born, Jesus showed up and talked with his folks, saying, "Your son will belong to God in a special way from the day he's born." Jesus gave the parents very specific instructions. As a sign of the boy's devotion to God, he wasn't supposed to drink wine or ever, ever cut his hair. Now there's nothing wrong with short hair, long hair, or in-between hair, but this was a way to show that Samson was set apart for God to use in a special way. When he grew up, he would become really strong. Like superhero strong. Think Superman. And the Hulk. And Thor.

Samson's father, Manoah, asked the angel of the Lord (remember, that's Jesus), "What is your name? When what you've said comes true, we want to give you the credit."

"Why do you ask my name?" Jesus said. "It is too wonderful for you to understand." That was kind of a funny response. You'd think this angel of the Lord would have given his name as Jesus because the specific name "Jesus" simply means

↖ Samson, the hero!

"God saves." But Jesus was getting at the fact that the totality of God's name (and all his name stands for) is so amazing it can't be wholly grasped. That means Jesus' code name is Magnificent. As in Awesome. Brilliant. Fantastic. Phenomenal.

"Gigantic," added Jo-Jo.

"Breathtaking," said Zuri-Claire, and the kids just kept going till we ran out of words.

In response to that name, Manoah and his wife offered a sacrifice to the Lord. Flames from the altar shot up toward the sky, and Jesus ascended in the fire. No special effects. This was real.

Samson was born and grew up, and he did some good things for Israel, mostly by accident while he was trying to get what he wanted. The enemies that were making Israel's life miserable during that time were the Philistines, and they did not like Samson. At all. And the feeling was mutual. Once, Samson caught 300 foxes, tied their tails together in pairs, attached a torch to each pair, and set them loose in the Philistines' fields—right at harvesttime! It wasn't very nice to the foxes, but it sure ticked off the enemy.

Another time, Samson picked up the jawbone of a donkey and killed 1,000 enemy soldiers in one fell swoop. *Blam!*

Another time, Samson picked up a city's gates and carried them off on his back. *Grrr.* The Philistines were so mad, and they tried every which way to kill him.

But Samson had a weakness. He liked a woman named Delilah who wasn't very nice. The Philistines who lived nearby offered Delilah a stack of money to find out the secret of Samson's strength.

Delilah tried everything. She nagged and nagged and nagged, but Samson wouldn't tell her. He tried tricking her, but she kept nagging. Finally, she wore him down, and he told her the truth. Delilah lulled him to sleep with his head in her lap, called a barber to chop off his hair, and hollered to his enemies.

"Samson!" Delilah shouted. "The Philistines are here!" Samson woke up and expected to beat down his enemies like he'd done before. But the strength of the Lord had left Samson. This time he was weak. The Philistines tied him up with ropes, gouged out his eyes to make him blind, and threw him in prison where he was forced to grind grain, day after day after day.

A funny thing happened in prison. I guess Samson had learned his lesson, because as his hair started to grow back, the strength of the Lord returned to him. But nobody knew about it except Samson.

One day, the Philistines threw a big party to honor their evil idol. The leaders brought out Samson to make fun of him. They'd forgotten about his hair, and by now it was pretty long.

Samson, the normal dude, before they poked his eyes out.

Samson asked a servant to guide him to the two big pillars that supported the temple roof. Samson pushed hard against the two pillars, the roof collapsed, and all the Philistines in the temple were crushed like bugs under your shoe—along with Samson. In his death, he scored a big victory over the enemies of Israel.

So that was Samson. Kind of a mixed-up dude, but God still worked through him.

Speaking of people getting crushed by falling temples, and other violent deaths, we're heading to the story about a fiery furnace built to burn people alive—which isn't cool at all. But something amazing happened in there, as we'll soon find out.

Samson's story reminds us to watch out for our weaknesses. Always stay the course. Make sure our weaknesses never push us off the path of being devoted to God.

See you hipsters next week.

KIRBY'S NOTES

STICK INSIDE YOUR BRAIN

"Why do you ask my name?" the angel of the LORD replied. "It is too wonderful for you to understand."

JUDGES 13:18

WANNA READ MORE?

Judges 13
Hebrews 11:32-40
Isaiah 9:6

14.
JESUS IN FLASH-FORWARD

Man, I musta wrote Zuri-Claire 12 million notes and crumpled them all. What am I supposed to say to her? "Hi, Kirby here. I think you're smart and funny and nice and cute and . . . blah, blah." She'll just laugh at me. Today she walked into junior church ahead of me, and I said hi again, and she kinda glanced at me like she might say hi back. But just then Aggy walked up and winked. I went red and turned away quick.

Okay, gotta teach.

There's nothing like a David harp solo.

Ahem.

Fast-forward a bunch of years. Israel eventually got kings, the first being Saul, a so-so kind of king, who did some good-king things and some not-so-great-king things. The next king was David. He made big mistakes but was also called "a man after God's own heart," because he was sorry about his mistakes and really wanted to obey God. The prophet Samuel predicted that Jesus would directly descend from King David.

King David liked to write poems and stuff, and a bunch of his poems were collected in a book called Psalms. David didn't write all the psalms in Psalms, but he wrote a lot of psalms in Psalms, so a lot of psalms in Psalms are David psalms but not all psalms in Psalms are. (Say that five times fast.)

Many psalms refer to Jesus indirectly, talking about Jesus' works or predicting Jesus' coming or how Jesus would die on the cross and come alive again and someday rule the universe. Other than Jesus, David was Israel's greatest king, hands down, but as far as we know, David never had a Christophany, one of those meetings with visible Jesus before he came to earth. But David had lots of God-given knowledge that predicted things about Jesus, and he wrote messianic psalms about him. Okay, vocab lesson: *messianic* means "about the Messiah," and *Messiah* is one of Jesus' titles. It means "Anointed One."

Some of David's knowledge went way beyond how you can ace a math test by studying hard or even how your mom knows amazing stuff because she has eyes in the back of her head.

It coulda worked like this: David would be writing a song, maybe to play on his harp and sing at the next family dinner, then something would click, and he'd think, *Whoa! Where did that come from?* He'd write and write, and what came out were his own words, but more than that—they were God's words too. David was tuned in to a direct channel, getting truth straight from God. Brainy scholars call this *inspiration*. It's a super-cool thing God did when he gave people the power, using their own thoughts, to write exactly what God wanted written. Sometimes they even wrote things way beyond natural thoughts, and brainy scholars call that *revelation*—a supercool thing God does where he makes known to people things they could never discover on their own.

Like when David wrote in Psalm 22, "All my bones are out of joint . . . they have pierced my hands and feet . . . they divide my garments among themselves and throw dice for my clothing," David's not talking about himself. He went through rough stuff, but nothing like that. He was exactly describing what Jesus would go through many years in the future. Jesus' bones were thrown out of joint from that crucifixion torture, and his hands and feet were pierced with nails as they hammered him onto the cross. Then the soldiers played a silly gambling game to see who'd get his clothes. God revealed those exact details to David hundreds of years before.

David was just one Bible writer who experienced writing down exactly what God wanted written. The New Testament explains, "All Scripture is inspired by God and is useful to teach us what is true and to make us realize what is wrong in our lives. It corrects us when we are wrong and teaches us to do what is right."

Grandpa McCook, shining his glasses on his shirttail and leaning forward in his recliner, grinned and said, "Yup! That's why we're so crazy about the Bible. It's God's very own words."

King David's son Solomon came next as king of Israel. Solomon started out wise—God gave him "a wise and understanding heart such as no one else has had or ever will have"—but as years went on, not so much. Like, one dumb thing he did was to marry hundreds and hundreds of wives—all at the same

KIRBY'S NOTES

STICK INSIDE YOUR BRAIN

All Scripture is inspired by God and is useful to teach us what is true and to make us realize what is wrong in our lives. It corrects us when we are wrong and teaches us to do what is right.

2 TIMOTHY 3:16

WANNA READ MORE?

2 Peter 1:20-21
Psalm 22:1-18
Isaiah 53

time. I mean, how are you ever going to have a romantic dinner together, just the 701 of you?

Even worse, almost all of Solomon's wives worshiped idols, and as the years went by, Solomon started worshiping idols too. DUMB! Big dummy doing dumb things! When people started worshiping idols—that was pretty much the end of good times for the nation of Israel. Things crumbled fast.

After Solomon died and his son took over, the nation split in two. A bunch of different kings ruled over the next years, some good, but most rotten. The two new kingdoms were called Israel and Judah—and eventually both of them got conquered. Israel fell to Assyria in 722 BC, and Judah fell to Babylon in 586 BC. People from Israel were force marched to Assyria, and people from Judah were hauled off to Babylon.

But God didn't desert them. He showed up even in their exile, as we'll see next week.

15.
JESUS KEEPS HIS COOL

"EW!!!!" yelled everybody as we came into the classroom.

Yucky worms sat on every chair.

Jimmy and Jayden were chortling. We caught on quick—these critters were actually gummy worms.

Zuri-Claire stared at the two perps, picked up her worm, and popped it into her mouth, just as cool as that. Then everybody laughed and did the same.

But how do I get this bunch to settle down?

Ahem.

Anybody here named Hananiah, Mishael, or Azariah? How about Stink Breath? Hey, that got your attention!

These three guys had wild names that also had cool meanings. Hananiah, Mishael, and Azariah mean "God is gracious," "Who is equal to God?," and "God has helped." They were friends of a brilliant young Hebrew, Daniel, whose name means "God is my judge." They were all carted off to Babylon, where the king hoped to brainwash them so they'd become loyal Babylonians and happily work for him.

The chief of staff under Babylon's King Nebuchadnezzar gave them new Babylonian names with really lame meanings. Daniel was called Belteshazzar, meaning "the false god Bel protects my life." Hananiah was called Shadrach, "commander of the moon god." Mishael got Meshach, "who is like the moon-god?" And Azariah got Abednego, "servant of the false god Nebo." Old Nebuchadnezzar was determined to make them forget the true God.

But Daniel and his pals followed God and did right, which was not easy in Babylon. Nebuchadnezzar was a huge show-off and built this ginormous statue of HIMSELF, 90 feet tall and 9 feet wide. He gave a wacko order that whenever his band's horns blasted and the flutes fluted and the trombones tromboned, everybody must fall to the ground and worship the gold statue—or *else!*

I mean, is that crazy or what?! The music plays, and idol worship follows?! I wonder if this band was named the Babylonian Beboppers. Maybe the Babylon Beatles. The Babylonian Beliebers?

But Daniel's friends said, "Nope, not gonna fall down and worship a dumb statue." (I'm pretty sure Daniel would have agreed, but he's not in this part of the story. Daniel had become an important official in Babylon, so he was probably away on a government mission.)

Anyhoo, King Neb got really ticked and ordered Shadrach, Meshach, and Abednego to come see him. He sneered, "So, you're not worshiping my statue, huh? If you don't do what I say, then I'm going to burn you alive. What god will be able to save you from my hands?"

They answered, "Sorry, King. We only worship God—and you ain't God. If we're thrown into the fiery furnace, the God we serve is able to save us. But even if God doesn't, we will never worship your golden statue."

The king got so mad his face squished up like a raging raccoon, and he ordered his men to heat the furnace seven times hotter than usual. He ordered his strongest muscle-bound guards to tie up the three Hebrews and throw them into the blazing furnace. In they went, ropes and all. The fire was so raging hot that it burned up the muscle-bound dudes who threw our guys in.

It really looked like God's plan to build a nation was all washed up. Or all burned up. The Israelites had lost their own land, and these few who loved God were about to die, so how was the Savior ever going to come from these people?!?!?

That's when Jesus entered the story.

The king was all set to toast some marshmallows on a super, super long stick when he stopped, looked deep into the fire, and exclaimed, "Hey—who's the wise guy around here who can't count?! Didn't we throw THREE men into the furnace?"

His advisers whipped out calculators and did the math. "Uh, yeah. Three is the right answer."

"Imbeciles! Look!" the king roared. "I see FOUR men walking around in the furnace. No ropes. They're not burning up. And the fourth man looks like a god!!!"

The king's advisers were all like, "Uh, sorry, King. Our calculator batteries just died."

See, it was Jesus in the fire with the three friends, keeping it real, keeping it cool. And that's a real cool, comforting thought, if you ask me.

Nebuchadnezzar came as close as he dared to the furnace door and shouted, "Dudes! Servants of the Most High God, come out!" So Shadrach, Meshach, and Abednego stepped out, and everybody crowded around. Guess what? They weren't burnt at all. Not a single hair on their heads was singed—and they didn't even smell like smoke.

Nebuchadnezzar changed his tune and ordered everybody not to say anything bad about the God of Shadrach, Meshach, and Abednego. If they did, then they'd be torn limb from limb and their houses smashed. Ol' King Neb never did anything halfway. The king announced, "There is no other god who can rescue like this!"

The three friends got promotions and lived happily ever after. Well, as happily as three dudes in captivity in Babylon could live. One thing didn't change—they followed God wholeheartedly all the days of their lives. And that's cool!

Remember, if somebody gives an order that God wouldn't like, then don't do it—even if you're thrown into a fiery furnace.

See you footloose freewheelers next week.

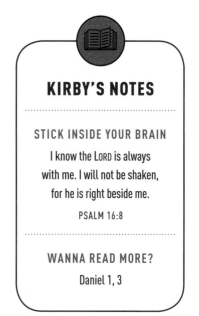

KIRBY'S NOTES

STICK INSIDE YOUR BRAIN
I know the Lord is always with me. I will not be shaken, for he is right beside me.
PSALM 16:8

WANNA READ MORE?
Daniel 1, 3

16.
JESUS AND A HOT-FUDGE SUNDAE

Dear Zuri-Claire,

I think you're cool.

Sincerely, Kirby

That's what I wrote. I gave the note to Emma, who gave it to Olivia, who gave it to Aggy, who gave it to Aisha, who gave it to—

OH NO!!!!!!

Jimmy just intercepted the note!!!!!!! Hoo man, I'm doomed. He'll read it out loud to everybody. I gotta do something. Gotta distract Jimmy! Gotta teach—RIGHT NOW!!!!!

↖ I HAD to prepare for this week's lesson.

AHEM!!!

Toward the end of the Old Testament, the coming of Jesus is predicted a bunch more times by people called prophets. These were folks who went around giving others messages straight from God.

The prophets focused a lot on the idea of longing for Jesus—not an idea kids talk about much these days. Maybe you LONG for your birthday to come, or LONG for a loved relative to visit. Maybe you LONG for a triple-decker hot-fudge sundae with extra whipped cream. When we LONG for something, it means we eagerly hope for it to arrive. The prophets really longed for Jesus, really looked forward to when he'd come to earth as the Messiah, the one who'd save the world.

Jimmy just sneezed on the note. He was reading it, and a big Ha-Ha-Ha-HA-HACHOOO exploded out of his nose all over it, and he wiped his old honker with MY NOTE!!!

MY NOTE FOR ZURI-CLAIRE!!!!

Can't let myself get distracted.

Ahem.

One prophet who longed for Jesus and wrote a lot about looking forward to seeing him was Isaiah. He predicted that Jesus will rule from Jerusalem one day. Like the chief justice of a world supreme court, he'll settle international disputes. The world will be at peace then, and instead of going to war, people will hammer their swords and spears into tools for plowing and planting. Probably that means tanks, guns, nuclear bombs, and even lightsabers will become tractors and combines and other farming tools to help grow food, because there won't be any wars to fight.

Once, in a vision of heaven, Isaiah saw the Lord seated on a throne—a pretty amazing sight. Angels surrounded the throne, each with six wings, and called out to each other: "Holy, holy, holy is the LORD of Heaven's Armies! The whole earth is filled with his glory!"

Their voices shook the building to its foundations and filled it with smoke. And Isaiah said, "It's all over! I'm doomed. I'm a sinful man with filthy lips, and I live around a whole bunch of people with filthy lips. Yet I've seen the LORD of Heaven's Armies."

An angel flew to Isaiah with a burning coal from the altar and touched him on the lips. "Don't worry," the angel said. "Your sins are forgiven."

Later, Isaiah was told that a virgin would have a child, and the name of the baby would be Immanuel, meaning "God with us." This is exactly what Jesus fulfilled when he came to us. He was born of a virgin, Mary, and Jesus was God on earth.

Hundreds of years before it happened, Isaiah told how Jesus wouldn't look like a regular king when he came to earth. He wouldn't appear majestic, wearing royal robes and stuff. Instead, he would be disliked, misunderstood, and rejected, a king who knew what grief was all about. He'd be crushed for our sins, beaten so we could be whole, whipped so we could be healed.

Ultimately, although the crushing and beating and whipping was totally bad, it was going to be a good day, because Jesus' suffering would mean that sins could be pardoned, sad days would eventually end, and the glory of the Lord would be revealed.

Another prophet, Malachi, predicted that a messenger would come ahead of Jesus to announce him. The prophet Micah pinpointed the exact spot where Jesus would be born, the little town of Bethlehem. The prophet Zechariah predicted that Jesus would ride into Jerusalem in triumph on a donkey, his side would be pierced, he'd be betrayed, and he'd be sold for thirty pieces of silver. Yep, centuries before it happened, the exact price was named.

The prophet Daniel predicted that Jesus would come to earth, not just once, but twice. And Hosea predicted that Jesus would spend a season in Egypt.

If all this sounds like really good news, it is—and that's only a fraction of what the prophets said about Jesus. But there's one prophecy that's really bad news. The prophet Jeremiah spoke it, and it's big-time horrible. It involves blood and guts and sorrow—and there's nothing funny about it at all. I want you to be prepared, because I'll tell you about it soon. So brace yourselves.

For now, remember: lots of people really looked forward to Jesus' first coming. And Jesus is going to come again. Are you looking forward to his second coming? No one except God knows the date, but it could be any day now.

See you next week. Unless . . .

KIRBY'S NOTES

STICK INSIDE YOUR BRAIN
Holy, holy, holy is the LORD of Heaven's Armies! The whole earth is filled with his glory!

ISAIAH 6:3

WANNA READ MORE?
Isaiah 2:3-4
Isaiah 7:14
Micah 5:2

17.
JESUS AND HIS COUNTRY COUSIN

Ha!! That note never got to Zuri-Claire!!! Good thing, because it was COMPLETELY GROSS. I guess Jimmy didn't get far in reading it, because after he sneezed and wiped his nose with it, he crumpled it and threw it in the trash. Whew!

But now I gotta write another note.

A better one. What do you think I should write?

Soooooooo gross!

Ahem.

Four hundred years went by with Jesus not showing up in person and with no prophets getting any more words from God. People were just supposed to keep reading and believing the words they already had.

Remember I told you a horrible thing is coming? But first, a really cool thing happens. And to get from here to there, we'll look at a guy with a really boring middle name—John THE Baptist. I mean, how crazy would it be if I was called Kirby THE McCook??

John's parents were named Zechariah and Elizabeth. They were both descended from Jewish priests, and they both followed God wholeheartedly.

Zechariah and Elizabeth were old folks—like Grandpa McCook old—and they'd never had a baby. They both wanted one, but figured it was never going to happen now. Zechariah worked as a priest, and one day he was serving God in the Temple. It was his turn—the opportunity of his lifetime, because there were so many priests he'd probably never get a turn again—to enter the Lord's sanctuary and burn incense. A big crowd stood outside and prayed.

While Zechariah was inside, an angel appeared to him and said, "Don't be scared, Zechariah. God's heard your prayers. Your wife, Elizabeth, will have a son, and you need to name him John. He'll be filled with the Holy Spirit even before his birth, and he'll prepare people for the coming of the Lord."

Zechariah was like, "Um, wow, but I'm an old geezer—and my wife is no spring chicken. It's pretty doubtful that we could have a baby."

The angel said, "I'm Gabriel! From the very presence of God! He sent me to bring you this good news. But since you didn't believe it, you won't be able to speak until your kid is born."

Sure enough, Zechariah came out of the Temple and couldn't speak. He could only wave his hands and play charades to tell people what happened. They didn't get it. But soon, Elizabeth became pregnant. They both were really happy about that, although Zechariah only said, "Mmmfff, armmm, shaa."

Meanwhile, not far away in Nazareth, a tiny village nobody cared about in the region of Galilee, lived Elizabeth's cousin Mary. Mary was already engaged to a dude named Joseph.

Mary and Joseph were swell folks, both descendants of King David, but not kings or queens or anything. Joseph worked as a craftsman, building tables and chairs and probably boxes to keep stuff in and maybe wheels for go-carts.

The same angel—Gabriel—appeared to Mary and said, "Hello there, favored woman! The Lord is with you. Don't be afraid—I'm here to say that you're going to have a baby boy. He'll be great. His name will be Jesus. God will give Jesus the throne of his ancestor David—and Jesus' Kingdom will never end!"

Mary was like, "What?! Who?! How?! I'm not even married yet. How can I have a baby?"

Gabriel responded, "Don't worry. The Holy Spirit will arrange it all, and the baby will be holy and will be the Son of God."

Mary said, "Okay, then. I'm God's servant. Whatever God wants for me is what I want too."

Mary went to Judea to visit her cousin Elizabeth. Mary walked through the doorway and said hi, and the baby inside Elizabeth's womb jumped for joy. Mary just burst out in song: "Wahoo—praise the Lord!! He fills the hungry with good things and remembers his promise to our ancestors."

Mary stayed with Elizabeth about three months. They probably talked a lot about baby stuff. Then Mary went home.

Elizabeth's baby was born. All the neighbors thought the baby would be named Zechariah, after his dad, because that's what people did back then. But old man Zechariah, who still couldn't speak, waved his hands for something to write on and wrote, "The kid's name is JOHN!"

Which surprised everybody. But instantly, Zechariah could speak, and the first thing he said was, "Praise God!" Then he added, "God has visited and redeemed his people and sent us a mighty Savior. And you, my little son, will prepare the way for the Lord."

KIRBY'S NOTES

STICK INSIDE YOUR BRAIN

Mary responded, "Oh, how my soul praises the Lord. How my spirit rejoices in God my Savior!"

LUKE 1:46-47

WANNA READ MORE?

Luke 1

John 1:14-15

And Baby John probably thought, "Mmmm, I'm so hungry I could eat a grasshopper."

Later John developed a real taste for grasshoppers, because he spent a lot of time out in the wilderness. We'll learn more about that soon. Don't you just want to eat a big old grasshopper?! Yum. So juicy.

18.
JESUS IS GOD FLESH-WRAPPED

Ever since Zuri-Claire ate the gummy worm, whenever I'm close by, like when we walk into class, I say, "Hey, Squirmy." (Get it? Squirmy Wormy?) She gives me this little half grin.

Ahem.

Dudes, let's get started.

Did I tell you that in those days Rome ruled everything? We studied the Roman Empire in history class, and those guys pretty much conquered the whole world. Rome did some good stuff, but they weren't exactly nice guys. The big-shot ruler of Rome back then was a guy named Caesar Augustus.

Israel was kind of like one of Rome's states in those days, and a guy named Herod was in charge there. Herod had a nasty temper, although he built some cool colossal stuff like water systems, a temple expansion, and a huge mountaintop fortress called Masada. Grandpa McCook has actually climbed that mountain.

Heads swiveled, and kids stared at Grandpa, who had taken off his clip-on tie and was getting settled in his chair.

"Well, I was younger then," Grandpa said.

The kids all stared even harder, and I could almost hear the calculators going in their heads—like—exactly how old ARE you?

"No, I wasn't there in Herod's day," Grandpa said. "I climbed Masada a few years ago and saw some of Herod's fortress that archaeologists have dug up. I'll show you my pictures one day."

Heads swiveled back around to me.

Folks did the best they could to live normal lives under this government of tyranny. They worked their jobs and rocked their babies and built their houses and tried to put food on the table. Throughout Israel, the longing for a Savior got even stronger. Lots of people hoped he'd come and just save them from Rome—they didn't quite get the big picture.

Here's a "younger" Grandpa McCook climbing a mountain that is NOT Masada.

When Mary left her cousin Elizabeth's house and got home to Nazareth, Joseph was like, "What's up with Mary?! How come she's pregnant but we're not married yet?!" But he was a kind dude and didn't want to embarrass Mary in any way, so he quietly planned to break off the engagement.

Then an angel showed up in a dream Joseph had and said, "Don't worry, Joe. It's okay to get married to Mary—and that's exactly what you should do next—soon. The baby is from the Holy Spirit. It's a boy, and you should name him Jesus, because that name means *Savior*, and he will save people from their sins."

Save? Even in his dream, Joseph's ears must have pricked up. He was a good Jewish man who knew about the prophecies of a Savior, and he knew the Savior would come through their nation. Could this be it?

So Joseph did as the angel told him. When he woke up, he married Mary, and it was just like the prophet Isaiah had said way back when: "A virgin will have a child, and the name of the baby will be 'Immanuel'" (meaning "God with us").

Maybe at this point you're wondering, if Jesus has been around forever, since before the beginning of time, and if Jesus has already done all these cool things like wrestle with Jacob and walk around in a fiery furnace with Shadrach, Meshach, and Abednego, how can Jesus also be born as a baby?

Yep, Jesus came into the very world he created—as one of us. The big word here is *incarnation*.

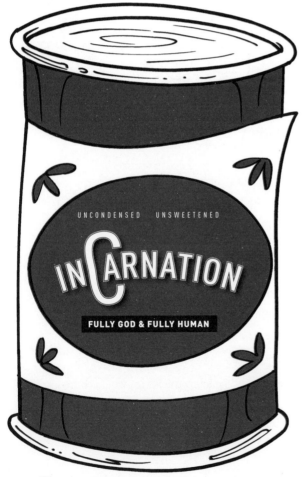

"*That's just a brand of condensed milk,*" *hollered Jimmy.*

I answered, "Sorry, noodle-brain, you got it wrong."

Incarnation means God became a human being and made his home right here on earth among us. He humbled himself and wrapped himself in flesh. God became a man, and Jesus is fully God at the same time that he's fully human.

That's good news.

For now, get this: the real, historic person known as Jesus Christ is also fully God. Jesus is far more than our buddy or our friend or a good teacher or just an example for us to follow. He's the Awesome Infinite Ruler of the Universe!

Okay, see you bunch of super-duper troopers next week.

KIRBY'S NOTES

STICK INSIDE YOUR BRAIN

The Good News is about his Son. In his earthly life he was born into King David's family line, and he was shown to be the Son of God when he was raised from the dead by the power of the Holy Spirit. He is Jesus Christ our Lord.

ROMANS 1:3-4

WANNA READ MORE?

Matthew 1:18-25
John 1:1, 10, 14
Philippians 2:5-8

19.
JESUS WAS AN ITTY-BITTY BABY

Dear Zuri-Claire,

Roses are red.
Violets are blue.
Skateboards are cool.
And so are you.

That's what I wrote the second time around. I'm so stinking poetic. Old Shakespeare has nothing on me.

I gave my note to Emma, who gave it to Olivia, who gave it to Aggy, who gave it to Aisha, who gave it to Zuri-Claire.

She's reading it now. She's kinda frowning. Or maybe she's just concentrating. Hoo man, maybe I wrote too much. I shouldn't let on that I like her that much!!!!! I'll start teaching quick—

Ahem.

Um, you guys are looking better than I expected. Nice tie, Mason.

The big-shot ruler of Rome, Caesar Augustus, said everybody must be counted in a census. To get the job done, you had to go to the town your ancestors were from.

Remember Joe? He was a descendant of King David, who was from Bethlehem, so he had to go there. He took along Mary, who was almost ready to give birth. When they got to Bethlehem, all the hotels and motels and hip bed-and-breakfasts were full, so they had to stay in a barn—or it might have been a cave, or a courtyard where animals lived, or even a travelers' shelter, kind of like a truck stop. And then all of a sudden Mary was like, "Ooooooh, Joe—it's time! This baby's coming!!! Boil hot water!"

And Joseph was like, "Ga-aaah! I'm gonna be a proud papa!!!"

Sure enough, the baby was born. Mary had strips of cloth to wrap him in, like good moms of that time did, but the only thing that looked like a crib was a food box for cows and horses and such, so they put the baby there, probably with a bunch of hay for softness.

I don't know if you've ever seen a newborn baby, but I saw my littlest sister soon after she was born. A baby is all pink and gooey, its face scrunched up, and it's either scream-ing or sleeping, and that's exactly what Jesus was doing. The Supreme Creator of the Universe was lying in a manger, being a baby. Wow. He probably waved his tiny hands around and maybe Joseph stuck out his pinky finger and Jesus grabbed hold the way babies do—those same mighty hands that had hurled stars into space and hung planet Earth in the sky.

That same night, a bunch of shepherds were out in a field, keeping their sheep out of trouble. Back then, shepherds had this reputation for being scruffy and dirty, and you'd think that when the Supreme Creator of the Universe was born, it would have been announced to important people. Maybe to Caesar Augustus and all the big shots and top dogs of the day. But nope, Jesus' birth was first announced to those scruffy, dirty shep-herds. Just regular folks with a bunch of regular sheep.

An angel from heaven appeared in the sky, and the radiance of the Lord lit up the place like a thousand bonfires, and the shepherds were totally scared and probably fell to the ground.

But the angel said, "Don't worry. I bring you good news that's going to bring great joy to lots of people. The Savior of the world has been born today in Bethlehem. You'll find him in a barn, wrapped in poor-people clothes, lying in a food trough made for animals."

Suddenly, the angel was joined by a huge pack of angels, all the armies of heaven— and they all praised God, saying, "Glory to God in highest heaven, and on earth peace and goodwill toward folks everywhere."

The sky went dark again, and the shepherds jumped to their feet and said, "We gotta go see this!" They hurried to Bethlehem and found Mary and Joseph. And sure enough, there was the baby, lying in the manger. They oohed and aahed—and *awed* (see what I did there?)—at baby Jesus, then went back to their flocks, praising God for what they'd seen and heard. They probably never got over it.

Not long after, some wise dudes from eastern lands saw the star of Jesus in the night-time sky. They followed the star all the way to Jerusalem, then asked around, "Where is the newborn king of the Jews?"

Remember super-rotten King Herod? Well, he heard that the wise men were asking around for a new king of the Jews, and he got super freaked out. So he called all the priests and other religious dudes together and asked them where the Messiah was supposed to be born.

"Bethlehem," the religious dudes said. "Duh."

Then that sewer rat King Herod said to the wise men, "You're looking for the king of the Jews? Me, too." (He probably smiled a big fake smile full of yellow teeth and bad breath, because—sure—he was looking for Jesus, but not to bring him baby gifts. Herod had something completely different up his dirty sleeve.) "Hey, why don't you guys go to Bethlehem and look, and when you find the kid, come back and tell me, so I can go worship him too. You know how folks always call me 'Uncle Herod'? BECAUSE I JUST LOVE BABIES."

Nope! Stinking, rotten, dirty liar!

We'll find out what happened next week.

KIRBY'S NOTES

STICK INSIDE YOUR BRAIN

I bring you good news that will bring great joy to all people. The Savior—yes, the Messiah, the Lord—has been born today in Bethlehem, the city of David! And you will recognize him by this sign: You will find a baby wrapped snugly in strips of cloth, lying in a manger.

LUKE 2:10-12

WANNA READ MORE?

Luke 2:1-20
Matthew 2:1-7

20.
JESUS ESCAPES THE NOOSE

I'm going bonkers wondering what Zuri-Claire thought of my note. I wish I'd said other things. No clue yet.

Ahem.

Well, the wise men from the east went to Bethlehem and found Jesus. They were super-ultra-happy to see him, and they gave Jesus presents of gold, frankincense, and myrrh—valuable stuff. When it came time to leave, God warned them in a dream not to return to Herod. Smart guys that they were—they weren't called wise men for nothing—they took another road home.

Joseph had a dream from God too. An angel of the Lord appeared to him and said, "Get up and run! Head through the desert to Egypt with the child and Mary and stay there until I tell you." So Joseph, Mary, and Jesus sneaked away in the dark, leaving that very night, which fulfilled another prophecy: that Jesus would go to Egypt. And they outwitted the old fox Herod, although he didn't know it for a while.

In the meantime, Herod's not done with his evil schemes.

WARNING: These scenes may not be suitable for all members of your family.

King Herod had been majorly ticked off when he'd heard the eastern visitors talk about a star that signaled the birth of a Jewish king. Herod had always been really mega-paranoid about other people trying to take his throne. He even killed three of his sons because he thought they might be plotting against him. So when he heard about a new king of the Jews, he wanted to take him out too. He learned about the new king being born in Bethlehem from the priests, but he didn't know exactly where in Bethlehem, which is why he wanted the wise men to come back and tell him.

King Baby

When the wise men didn't report back, Herod threw a tantrum. He called up his soldiers and sent them to Bethlehem to kill all little boys two years old and under. That way, he figured he'd be sure to get Jesus. So that's what happened. Babies were slaughtered in Bethlehem. Remember how I told you the prophet Jeremiah had predicted blood and sorrow? Hundreds of years earlier, he'd said, "A cry was heard in Israel—weeping and great mourning. Mothers are weeping for their children. They refuse to be comforted, for the children are dead."

Yep, horrible, horrible story—and we don't know why God allowed such horror. I bet

God cried along with those mothers. Evil was and still is strong in the world, thanks to people freely choosing it, and that's why the world so desperately needs a Savior.

Well, the Savior, Jesus, was safely hidden away in Egypt. Herod died pretty soon after he'd killed all those kids, and the ancient historian Josephus records that Herod's death was excruciatingly painful. Everybody hated Herod—and he knew it. Herod worried nobody would mourn for him after he died, so right before his death, he ordered a large group of important leaders to be killed too—then everybody would be sad. Fortunately for those leaders, the order wasn't carried out. But that's how nutso Herod was.

Satan was really the one behind evil Herod, thinking here was his chance to win the great war with heaven. The devil had already squashed the nation God had built and had it under Roman rule, and at this time the Israelites were only one cut above slaves. Now the devil thought he could squash the long-promised Savior by wiping him out as a baby. Nope. The Savior was alive and well and growing up as a happy kid in Egypt!

Herod's son, Herod Archelaus, came to power, and then the angel appeared to Joseph again and told him to take Mary and Jesus and go home. They went to live in Nazareth, their little hometown in Israel.

Not much is known about Jesus' childhood, except that he grew up healthy and strong. When he was 12, same as me, Kirby McCook, he and his folks went to Jerusalem for the annual Passover celebration.

After the celebration, everybody headed home, but Jesus stayed behind. Folks often traveled in big groups back then, and his parents figured he was walking with the families of friends. But after a while they got concerned and went back to Jerusalem to look for him.

They found him in the Temple, talking with all the brainy religious teachers. The teachers listening to Jesus were amazed at his understanding.

"Hey, Son," said his mom, "we've been looking for you everywhere. You worried us. What gives?!"

"Didn't you know I needed to be at my Father's house?" Jesus said. It wasn't a bratty comeback, just the calm fact.

So that's how Jesus was born and grew up. He grew wiser by the day, just like he grew taller. God's favor was on him, and people liked him just fine.

Personally, I wonder if he ever ate a grasshopper. I've still got grasshoppers on my mind. Next we'll look at John the Baptist, the king of the grasshopper eaters.

For now, remember: Jesus, the Supreme Creator of the Universe, was also born as a baby.

See you bunch of peachy kids next week.

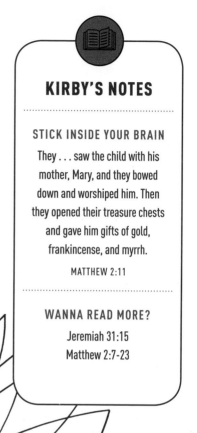

KIRBY'S NOTES

STICK INSIDE YOUR BRAIN

They . . . saw the child with his mother, Mary, and they bowed down and worshiped him. Then they opened their treasure chests and gave him gifts of gold, frankincense, and myrrh.

MATTHEW 2:11

WANNA READ MORE?

Jeremiah 31:15
Matthew 2:7-23

21.
JESUS MEETS THE GRASSHOPPER EATER

Hey, so Zuri-Claire is going to write me a note back. I heard this from Emma, who heard it from Olivia, who heard it from Aggy, who heard it from Aisha. They say ZC will write next week. Hoooo, I wonder what she'll say!

Ahem.

A few years passed. Jesus' cousin, John the Baptist, was sort of an outsider. Like, you might not want to invite him to your birthday party. Or maybe you would. It might be cool having a guy there wearing scratchy camel hair clothes and a leather belt, a dude used to hanging out in the desert. Hey there, hairy Sasquatch, how about a game of pin the tail on the donkey?

Besides the grasshopper munching, John ate lots of wild honey, and that was pretty much it for his snacks. He dunked lots of people in the Jordan River, baptizing them to show they'd repented of sin.

And he went around yelling a lot. He often yelled, "SOMEONE IS COMING SOON WHO IS GREATER THAN ME. HE'S BEEN AROUND SINCE BEFORE THE DAWN OF TIME, AND HE'S SO GREAT I'M NOT EVEN WORTHY TO BEND DOWN LIKE A SLAVE

AND UNTIE THE STRAPS OF HIS SANDALS. I BAPTIZE YOU WITH WATER, BUT HE WILL BAPTIZE YOU WITH THE HOLY SPIRIT."

I guess you've figured out that John's middle name wasn't really THE. He was called John the Baptist because of his work. Like Joseph the carpenter or Jimmy's dad the accountant.

Anyway, John's work was what Isaiah had predicted: "He's a voice SHOUTING in the wilderness, 'PREPARE THE WAY FOR THE LORD'S COMING! CLEAR THE ROAD FOR HIM!'"

John could get pretty tough on those he shouted at. One day, he looked at the crowd and yelled, "YOU BUNCH OF SNAKES! YOU THINK YOU'VE TURNED FROM YOUR SINS, BUT I'D LIKE TO SEE SOME FRUIT WITH YOUR REPENTANCE." By *fruit*, he didn't mean kumquats and kiwis. He meant doing good things.

That got their attention. Some said: "Uh, John, you're undoubtedly right. What should we do?"

He yelled, "IF YOU HAVE TWO PAIRS OF PANTS AND YOU SEE A DUDE IN HIS UNDERWEAR, THEN GIVE HIM A PAIR OF YOUR PANTS. IF YOU HAVE A BIG LUNCH AND SEE A GUY WHO'S HUNGRY, GIVE HIM FOOD."

"Oh," said the crowd. "That sounds reasonable. We can do that. At least sometimes."

Tax collectors hung around. These dudes often cheated the people they collected tax from by insisting the bill was higher. They said to John, "We know we're skunks. What should we do?"

John yelled: "PRETTY OBVIOUS, AIN'T IT?! JUST COLLECT WHAT YOU'RE SUPPOSED TO COLLECT—NO MORE. OKAY?!"

The crowds liked John, but one guy not so much. His name was Herod Antipas, aka Herod the Tetrarch. He was the son of Herod the Baby Killer and brother of Herod Archelaus.

The problem arose after Herod Antipas kicked out his first wife, Phasaelis, and married his half-brother's wife, Herodias, instead. John publicly criticized Herod Antipas for that—and for many other wrongs Herod Antipas did. That got John thrown into prison. *Bam!* Just like that. Herodias had a daughter named Salome who was a good dancer but seems to have had trouble thinking for herself. She'll factor into the story soon. But I'm getting ahead of myself.

Before John was tossed into prison, he was out one day baptizing people in the Jordan, and what do you know? His cousin, about 30 years old now, walked into the water to be baptized. John looked at Jesus and shouted to the crowd, "HEY, LOOK! IT'S THE LAMB OF GOD WHO TAKES AWAY THE SIN OF THE WORLD."

(Remember the Passover lamb—how the Hebrews in Egypt put the blood of an unblemished lamb on their doorposts, so the angel would pass over their house and their firstborn wouldn't die? Well, John was calling Jesus the ultimate Passover lamb. Someone who had the ability to erase the sins of the whole world.)

Jesus asked John to baptize him, but John said, "No way. I'm the one who needs to be baptized by you. Why would you come to me?"

"It's right for me to be baptized," Jesus said. "It fulfills all righteousness." (Grandpa McCook said most scholars think Jesus wanted to be baptized simply to identify with sinners. Sort of to come alongside us and show us that, even though he never did any sin, he could climb into the same boat with us.)

John baptized Jesus, and after Jesus came up out of the water, the sky split apart. The Spirit of God descended and settled on Jesus like a dove, and a voice from heaven said, "This is my dearly loved Son, who brings me great joy."

It was a pretty remarkable day all around, and Jesus went on a trip right afterward. It lasted for 40

KIRBY'S NOTES

STICK INSIDE YOUR BRAIN

The next day John saw Jesus coming toward him and said, "Look! The Lamb of God who takes away the sin of the world!"

JOHN 1:29

WANNA READ MORE?

Isaiah 40:2-5

Matthew 3

Luke 3:1-20

days and 40 nights and was no fun at all. I'll tell you about it soon. For now, remember: Jesus takes away the sins of the world.

Okay, see you solid kids next week.

22.
JESUS GETS DOWN TO BUSINESS

Zuri-Claire didn't write me a note. Sigh. Maybe next week . . .

Ahem.

Okay class, on with business. I told you that Jesus went on a trip, and it wasn't like any trip you'd ever see in a travel brochure. If you did, here's what the brochure would say:

ENJOY
40 DAYS AND 40 NIGHTS IN THE HOT DUSTY WILDERNESS

SLEEPING ACCOMMODATIONS:
BED OF ROCKS

FOOD:
NONE

ACTIVITY:
TEMPTATION BY THE DEVIL

The Holy Spirit led Jesus out to the bare hills. After 40 days and nights, Jesus got mighty hungry after going without food for so long, so he wasn't feeling great. Then the devil came to him and said, "Hey, if you're really the Son of God, then grab a bunch of rocks and *alakazam!* Turn those rocks into bread."

"NO WAY!" Jesus said. "The Scriptures say that people don't live by bread alone, but by every word that comes from the mouth of God."

Then the devil led Jesus into Jerusalem, up to the roof of the Temple, and said, "If you're really the Son of God, then jump off this roof without a parachute. Don't worry, the Scriptures say angels will protect you."

"NO WAY!" Jesus said. "Because the Scriptures also say, 'Don't test God.'"

"All right, all right," the devil whined. Then he took Jesus to a high mountain peak and showed him fancy loot from all the kingdoms of the world, saying, "It's all yours, Jesus. All you need to do is kneel down and worship me."

"NO WAY!" Jesus told him. "Get lost, Satan! The Scriptures say, 'You must worship the Lord your God and serve only him.'"

Then the devil left Jesus, and angels came and took care of him.

See, when it came to A) physical appetites and B) personal goals and C) an easy path to success, the devil wanted Jesus to do things the devil's way. Not God's way. But three times Jesus said NO WAY! to temptation. That's a good lesson for us. Next time we're tempted to do something wrong, remember God's plan and say NO WAY!

Soon after, Jesus traveled to the Sea of Galilee and went for a walk on the beach. Two brothers, Simon and Andrew, were hanging out there. They were both fishermen.

"Come follow me," Jesus said. "I'll show you how to fish for people."

Right away, the brothers left their nets and followed Jesus, who was lots more exciting than a bunch of stinky old fish. Jesus told Simon, "I've got a nickname for you. It's Peter."

Peter must have been a big, tough, burly dude, because his nickname means the Rock. Simon Peter the Rock. Later, Simon Peter's strong faith in the great truth of who

Jesus really was would become the rock on which Jesus built his church. But I'm jumping ahead.

Just up the beach were two other brothers that Jesus later nicknamed Sons of Thunder. Their real names were James and John, and they were also fishermen. They sat in a boat with their dad, Zebedee, repairing nets. Jesus called the Sons of Thunder to follow him, and right away they said, "See you later, Dad," and followed Jesus.

The next day Jesus found Philip and said, "Come, follow me."

"Will do," Philip said. "But I wish I had a cool nickname too." Philip went and found his buddy, Nathanael (sometimes called Bartholomew, which isn't a very cool nickname, really), and said, "We've found the very person Moses and the prophets wrote about. He's the Savior, and he's from Nazareth!"

"Nazareth?!" Nathanael said. "That smelly little town with the lousy reputation?! Nah, I don't think anything good can come from Nazareth!"

"Stop being so uptight," Philip said. "Come and see for yourself—Jesus is the real deal."

Nathanael was most likely a rich dude with the right education and great toys and too much free time on his hands. He was probably a bit stuck up, too. But he followed Jesus, and Jesus told Nathanael that he'd see far greater things than all his hoity-toity wealth. All these guys became the first of Jesus' disciples—his followers.

Did you know that we can be disciples of Jesus today? Although we don't literally walk around the land of Israel with Jesus, we can still follow his teachings. We can be his friends. We can be close to him. Jesus

KIRBY'S NOTES

STICK INSIDE YOUR BRAIN

Jesus called out to them, "Come, follow me, and I will show you how to fish for people!"

MATTHEW 4:19

WANNA READ MORE?

Matthew 4:1-11; 18-22
John 1:35-50
Luke 5:1-11; 27-32

can change our lives. Even today, we can go on a mission with Jesus to love people closer to God. That's what it means to follow Jesus.

Think about that this week.

23.
JESUS LIKES PARTIES

Hey, here's another reason why I like Zuri-Claire so much. Today, she brought CUPCAKES to class! She'd found out somehow that it's Grandpa McCook's 79th birthday.

We all sang to him, and he grinned and ate two or three cupcakes. (I had to sneakily wipe some frosting off his chin.)

I tried to tell Zuri-Claire thanks, but every time I looked at her, she kind of shyly looked away.

Ahem.

Okay, enough partying. We're going to find out today that Jesus liked parties too.

Some kids think it's boring to follow Jesus, but I dunno—the Jesus I follow is far from boring. The first miracle Jesus ever did was at a huge party—a wedding celebration—and in those days, a Jewish wedding lasted seven whole days. Imagine a party lasting a whole week!!!!!

There was lots of music and dancing and food, then more music and more dancing, and more food, food, food. And all kinds of wine, which kids today don't usually drink, of course. But back then their water supply was kinda gross, so they all drank a watered-down form of fermented grape juice (or maybe even fresh grape juice), and it was actually healthier than water because it didn't have bugs and germs and junk in it.

Anyhoo, toward the end of the party, the wine ran out, and the wedding host was totally embarrassed. Jesus' mom nudged Jesus in the ribs and said, "Hey, Son, do something." I guess Jesus' mom was not used to taking no for an answer, because then she turned to some servants and added, "Do whatever he tells you to do."

The host had six cold, clammy stone water jars used for cold, clammy religious rituals. They did these rites and ceremonies over and over in hopes of getting closer to God.

Jesus didn't want to make a scene, because it wasn't time yet to reveal that he was God the Son. He wanted to keep that exciting stuff under wraps a little longer. But he said simply to the servants, "Fill those six ceremonial jars to the top with water," and when the jars were full he added, "Now dip some out and take it to the dude in charge of the wedding."

"WAHOO!" the wedding dude said when he sipped the drink. "This is the BEST WINE I EVER TASTED!!" He beamed this huge smile. And on went the party.

Jesus had turned water into wine—and not the kind of wine they usually drank. This was superwine, an extremely tasty, refreshing, robust, life-giving, joy-filled wine that replaced the cold, clammy water used for religious rituals.

Grandpa McCook piped up, "That's just like Jesus, isn't it? He pushes away old boring religion and replaces it with a new kind of life—a life filled with freedom and joy and adventure." He nodded a couple times and brushed cupcake crumbs off his vest.

Jesus could get serious too. Really serious. A short while after the party, Jesus went to the Temple area. A bunch of folks had set up shops right in the Temple to sell all sorts of cows and sheep and doves for sacrifices. Originally, the businesses were probably just set up to be handy for people. But the whole area had turned into a sort of a circus with lots of money and greed flowing.

Jesus was ticked. When there's lots of money to be made, worship can easily become fouled up, and I guess that's what had happened, because he made a whip from some ropes and started cracking it.

"Get all those things out of here!" he yelled. "Don't you know this is my Father's house?!"

Hiss. Snap. Crack! went the whip.

Those two things—turning the water into wine and clearing the Temple—were the first two actions of Jesus' public ministry. For the next three years, Jesus traveled around to towns and villages in Israel. He taught lots of people lots of things, and he healed lots of people and told them lots of cool stories about the Kingdom of God.

Oh, you should know: the KINGDOM that Jesus was talking about was a spiritual kingdom of change in people's hearts, not a physical kingdom where he wore a crown and sat on an old uncomfortable throne. Lots of folks didn't understand this. But you do, right?

As they traveled, Jesus and his disciples had all sorts of adventures, and we'll get to more of those in a jiffy.

For now, remember: just like he turned cold, clammy water into rich, robust wine at a wedding, Jesus invites us to follow him and experience his joy and adventure.

KIRBY'S NOTES

STICK INSIDE YOUR BRAIN

[Jesus said,] "My purpose is to give them a rich and satisfying life."

JOHN 10:10

WANNA READ MORE?

John 2:1-16

24.

JESUS MEETS FOLKS ONE-ON-ONE

Zuri-Claire didn't write me a note this week either.

What is it with Zuri-Claire?

Why do I like her so much, even when she doesn't write me notes?!

I should do something while I wait. Maybe I should write HER another note. But it's her turn to write me. Sigh.

Ahem.

Hey there, kiddos.

Word got around, and lots of folks thought about what Jesus did at that party, and some whistled at what he did with that whip. Some wanted to meet with him privately.

Nicodemus, a sincere and important religious leader, came to Jesus one evening after dark. Nicodemus was elderly, and "after dark" wasn't a usual visiting time, given that he ate supper at 4:30 p.m. and went to bed at 7:00. Most likely, Nicodemus was scared other religious leaders might see him in the daylight, so he came after hours. He asked Jesus about what it meant to follow him.

"Well, you can't see the Kingdom of God unless you're born again," Jesus said.

"What do you mean, 'born again'?" Nicodemus asked. "I'm an old man. Should I become like an itty-bitty baby again and somehow go back into my mother's womb?"

"Nope," Jesus said. "Being born again is a spiritual thing."

"What's that supposed to mean?" Nicodemus asked.

Jesus explained that when you're born again, you're born spiritually into the family of God. He told Nicodemus: "This is how God loved the world: He gave his one and only Son, so that EVERYONE WHO BELIEVES in him will not perish but have eternal life." (Yep—that's John 3:16, one of the most famous verses in the Bible.)

We're pretty sure Nicodemus eventually chose to believe and follow Jesus, because later on, he helped out a dude named Joseph of Arimathea with Jesus' burial. But I'm jumping ahead.

One day, Jesus and his disciples traveled through the region of Samaria. Jesus was Jewish, and Jews and Samaritans often didn't get along. But God loves the whole world through Jesus—even Samaritans—so Jesus chose to spend time in Samaria and meet people there. In a village named Sychar, Jesus sat down beside a well and sent the disciples ahead to buy lunch. Probably not burgers and fries, but maybe bread and cheese and olives and dates.

It was noon, the hottest part of the day, and a Samaritan woman came to dip water from the well. Why noon? Because she liked being alone and nobody else came when the noon sun blazed. People made fun of her. See, she'd made some bad decisions, which she was embarrassed about, and if she came to the well at noon then she could be pretty sure she'd be alone. Clever.

Back then, men who were teachers didn't usually talk to women in public, unless they were married to them. So Jesus totally surprised this woman by saying, "Hey there, would you give me a drink of water, please?"

The woman said, "You're a Jew, and I'm a Samaritan woman. Why are you asking ME for a drink?"

That question led to a deeper conversation, where Jesus told her that God gave people gifts of "living water," and people who drank this living water would never be thirsty again. It was sort of a poetic way of saying, "Look, if you believe in me, your life will feel satisfied."

See, looking at the story, it seems pretty safe to conclude that this woman felt unsatisfied. She'd had five different husbands, and nope, this wasn't Hollywood. Maybe her husbands had died, or they were all rotten dudes, or maybe she was really choosy—we're not sure. Either way, Jesus told her that she'd been looking for love in all the wrong places. But God could satisfy the needs of her heart. Jesus said something like, "*Psst . . . I know about your five husbands,*" even before she admitted her life was a mess.

He probably said it with a warm smile, still offering living water. Well, this just blew the woman's mind, and she left her water jar beside the well, ran back to the village, and yelled up a storm: "Come and meet a man who told me everything I ever did! Could he be the Savior?"

A bunch of folks flocked from the village to see Jesus, and Jesus stayed with the Samaritans for two days, long enough for lots of folks to hear his message of Good News and believe in him.

Remember: we each need to meet Jesus for ourselves. If your parents and grandparents are all believers, that doesn't make you one. You still need to be born again and let Jesus satisfy your deepest needs.

KIRBY'S NOTES

STICK INSIDE YOUR BRAIN

This is how God loved the world: He gave his one and only Son, so that everyone who believes in him will not perish but have eternal life.

JOHN 3:16

WANNA READ MORE?

John 3:1-21

John 4:1-30

25.
JESUS IS NO PUSHOVER

Nope, nothing. My pockets are empty. Nothing tucked into my Bible case. Nothing slipped into my hand.

Ahem. Let's get started, dudes and dudettes.

After two days in Samaria, Jesus went on to Galilee to the village of Cana—remember, that's the town where he'd turned water into wine. A dude who worked for the government in the town of Capernaum, about a day's journey away, had a little boy who was very sick. The government dude went to Jesus and begged him to come to Capernaum and heal his son, who was at death's door by then.

"Just go on home," Jesus said. "Your son will live." Somebody checked their sundial and saw it was 1:00 p.m.

The man nodded and started heading home. That night passed and a new day began. Before the man reached home, his servants ran out to meet him and announced excitedly that his son was alive and not sick anymore.

"What time did he get better?" the man asked.

"Yesterday at 1:00 p.m.," they said.

Yep, that's the EXACT TIME Jesus had told him his son would get better. After that, the man and his household all trusted Jesus and whatever he said. They weren't dummies.

Jesus came to the village of Nazareth, where he'd grown up. He went to the synagogue (sort of like church) on the Sabbath (the day they worshiped) and stood up to read the Scriptures, a common practice back then. Any visitor could do that.

Somebody handed Jesus the scroll of the prophet Isaiah. Jesus unrolled the scroll and read:

> The Spirit of the LORD is upon me,
>   for he has anointed me to bring Good News to the poor.
> He has sent me to proclaim that captives will be released,
>   that the blind will see,
> that the oppressed will be set free,
>   and that the time of the LORD's favor has come.

Jesus rolled the scroll back up and said: "That's me. That's who Isaiah was talking about. I'm here to bring good news to the poor. I'm here to set captives free. I'm here so the blind will see. I'm here so people everywhere will be set free. The time of God's favor has come! The Scripture you've just heard has been fulfilled this very day!"

If anybody had been paying attention to this Scripture and had put it together with the amazing things Jesus had been doing, they would have caught on that Jesus was the promised Savior, God the Son.

But the people who heard Jesus that day in Nazareth just sort of murmured among themselves, kind of grumbling, "Yeah, but isn't this guy Joseph's son? Like, we all know Jesus, and we remember when he was just a kid, playing on the floor of the carpenter's shop, drinking root beer and eating fruit snacks. Now he's all grown up and saying he's fulfilled the prophecy of Isaiah. Really?"

Jesus said, "Hey, I know what you're thinking. But no prophet is ever accepted in his hometown."

Then the people got ticked at Jesus. Really ticked. A bunch of them jumped up and mobbed him. They shoved and kicked and moved as a group with Jesus right in their middle all the way out of town to the edge of a cliff.

"Throw him off!" someone yelled.

"Yeah!" someone else shouted. "Make him hurt!"

But Jesus did something—we don't know exactly what—maybe he gave them some kind of God-look. For sure, he did something that made everyone stop their shoving and yelling and take a half step back from Jesus. He passed right through the crowd away from the cliff and went on his way. Yep, Jesus was no pushover.

This wasn't the last time Jesus would get into a hairy situation—and we'll hear about a couple more soon.

For now, remember: God loves all types of people through Jesus—even those who are different from you, even doubters and grumblers, and especially those who are hurting.

Okay, see you later, skaters.

KIRBY'S NOTES

STICK INSIDE YOUR BRAIN

God showed his great love for us by sending Christ to die for us while we were still sinners.

ROMANS 5:8

WANNA READ MORE?

John 4:43-54

Isaiah 61:1-2

Luke 4:14-30

26.
JESUS MEETS SOME SICK DUDES

YOU'LL NEVER GUESS WHAT?!?!?

I can hardly believe it myself!! Zuri-Claire wrote me a note. She gave it to Aisha, who gave it to Aggy, who gave it to Olivia, who gave it to Emma, who gave it to me. It said:

Dear Kirby,
Do you like movies? Yes ___ No ___
Do you like books? Yes ___ No ___
Do you like ice cream? Yes ___ No ___
Do you like dogs? Yes ___ No ___

Sincerely,
Zuri-Claire

Wowee, that Zuri-Claire sure has a way with words.

Ahem. Hey there, class.

Did I tell you that Peter the Rock was married? We know that he was married because he had a mother-in-law who got very sick. She took to her bed with a high fever. You know how yucky you feel when your mom checks you with a thermometer and shakes her head and her mouth goes into a grim line? Well, this woman felt way worse.

"Please heal her," everyone begged, probably because they really liked her a lot.

Jesus simply went to her bedside, took her by the hand, and helped her sit up. Then Jesus rebuked the fever. What does it mean to "rebuke" something? Well, you scold it. You tell it, "Knock it off." That's what Jesus did with that fever. The fever left, and Peter's mother-in-law became perfectly healthy again. She got up and fixed them a meal, because that's what grandmas like to do and she knew they all had good healthy appetites.

Word got around about miracles like this that Jesus kept doing, and more and more people followed Jesus.

Okay, you need to know that one of the grossest, most feared diseases in those days was called *leprosy*. The disease caused a person to lose feeling throughout the body. So people would cut themselves and not know it. Or step into a fire without noticing and just let it burn till their foot smelled like barbecued monkey meat. Or they'd break an ankle but just keep walking on it until it filled with pus.

Leprosy is still around these days, although not many people get it. But if you were a leper in Jesus' day, you had to keep your distance from people and yell, "UNCLEAN! UNCLEAN!" because this horrid disease was really contagious. It was no way to live, said everyone who ever had it.

One man with an ugly case of leprosy didn't follow the rules. We don't know what he looked like, but if his leprosy was advanced then it's safe to say he was no picture postcard. I mean: nose missing. Eyeballs falling out of their sockets. No fingers. Only three teeth left. He walked right up to Jesus and knelt at his feet, and I bet you could hear the crowd gasp in horror.

"If you are willing," the man said, "you can heal me and make me clean."

Jesus felt compassion for the guy. He reached out and touched him. That was a crazy move right there, because back then, people didn't go around touching lepers. But Jesus didn't mind. He was going to help the man no matter what people thought.

"I'm willing," Jesus said. "Be healed." Instantly, the man was healed!

Wow, can you imagine that scene? *Poof!* Instantly, the guy's got a nose again. *Thu-thunk!* Eyeballs are back in their sockets. *Zip, zip, zip!* Fingers grow while you blink. The guy's clean! Healed!! All better!!!

Jesus told the former leper not to tell anyone who did this for him, but of course the man told everyone. The reports of Jesus' power spread faster and farther, and then the crowds grew bigger and bigger. Jesus wasn't trying to draw a big crowd—that's not what he was all about.

← right before his fingers fell off

He was never a show-off, and he also didn't want to draw the attention of the officials because that would mean big trouble.

After healing people, Jesus never made a big announcement. Instead, he often went away by himself so he could pray.

We'll see him meet some more oddballs next week.

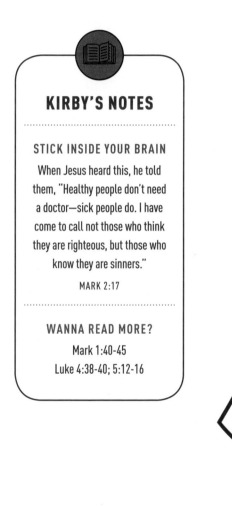

KIRBY'S NOTES

STICK INSIDE YOUR BRAIN

When Jesus heard this, he told them, "Healthy people don't need a doctor—sick people do. I have come to call not those who think they are righteous, but those who know they are sinners."

MARK 2:17

WANNA READ MORE?
Mark 1:40-45
Luke 4:38-40; 5:12-16

after Jesus healed him ⟶

27.
JESUS AND THE SLIMEBALLS

I need to think long and hard about each answer I give on Zuri-Claire's note before I send it back. How would you answer?

Ahem.

Let's go, tigers.

One day, Jesus was teaching in a house that was so packed not one more person could get inside. We're talking wall-to-wall people, belly-to-back, jammed tighttighttight.

Four friends had a buddy who couldn't walk. He was paralyzed and needed to be carried everywhere. The friends wanted to bring the dude to Jesus, but they couldn't get inside the house, so they improvised. They hefted their pal up to the roof, dug a hole through the ceiling, and lowered the man right down in front of Jesus. *Hello?! Who's this?!*

Jesus knew the friends had lots of faith. When they couldn't get through the front door, their faith was big enough to craft a crazy plan. Jesus said to the dude on his mat, "Son, your sins are forgiven."

Hey, that was a twist. The guy couldn't *walk*. So why did Jesus start by *forgiving the man's sins*? A bunch of gloomy religious teachers, listening, got all uppity about this. "Who does this Jesus fellow think he is?!" they said. "Only God can forgive sins."

Jesus could read their minds. He asked, "Hey, is it easier for a teacher to say, 'Your sins are forgiven?' Or is it easier to make a paralyzed guy walk again? What do you think?"

The gloomy guys said nothing, so Jesus continued, "Just so you understand what's going on here, watch this. I want you to know how I dare to forgive this guy's sins." Jesus turned to the man and added, "Stand up. Pick up your mat, and go home!"

Shu-shunk! The man jumped up, grabbed his mat, and walked out the front door. People were so stunned they stepped back and made a path. Everybody's jaws hung open. Then they all let loose at once and praised God. They'd never seen anything like it.

See, Jesus could tell the man his sins were forgiven, because Jesus had all authority in the matter. Jesus was God. Jesus could forgive sins, and Jesus could heal people. Both were easy for him—a mere snap of the fingers for someone who'd made the entire universe.

When Jesus left that town, he saw a dude named Levi. Everybody glared at Levi except Jesus. See, Levi was one of those slimeball tax collector guys nobody liked.

But Jesus walked right over to the cheater and said, "Hey there, Levi, follow me and be my disciple."

Levi thought this was a good idea. He left everything and followed Jesus.

Levi also went by the name Matthew, and later, Levi/Matthew threw a party in his home to honor Jesus. Levi invited a bunch of friends, and when you're a slimeball tax collector and everybody hates you, your only friends are other slimeball tax collectors.

People saw Jesus at the party with those guys, and some uptight religious folks said, "C'mon, Jesus, what's the matter with you?! You can do better than that. You're hanging out with scum."

Jesus said, "Think of me as a doctor. If you're healthy and happy, then you don't need a doctor. But if you're sick and miserable, then who you gonna call?" Jesus was always ready to hang out with people who needed him.

Even if they had high fevers.

Even if they were lepers or paralytics.

Even if they were slimeball tax collectors and dirty rotten scoundrels.

See, no matter what's got you down, Jesus wants to hang out with you. Grandpa McCook told me that all people have sinned and fallen short of God's glory. All. That means me and you, and your next-door neighbor, and your longtime friend who remembers all the embarrassing things you did in prekindergarten. We're all rowing the same sin boat together.

But God in his grace freely makes us right in his sight. He does this through Jesus when we believe in him.

See, apart from Jesus, we don't have power to live the way we're meant to live, and our lives are all broken and slimy in some way. But Jesus makes things the way they're supposed to be. Healed. Satisfied. Healthy again.

Nope—Jesus doesn't cure every fever, just like he didn't heal every leper or eat dinner with every tax collector. He did just enough to show us who he was, so we could make no mistake about it. The healing that Jesus GUARANTEES is inward and spiritual—and that's available to everyone at any time. And that's real cool.

Not everybody understood this about Jesus. Or liked him very much, as we'll hear soon.

For now, remember: Jesus makes all things new.

See you soon, you stellar kids.

KIRBY'S NOTES

STICK INSIDE YOUR BRAIN
We are made right with God by placing our faith in Jesus Christ. And this is true for everyone who believes, no matter who we are. For everyone has sinned; we all fall short of God's glorious standard.

ROMANS 3:22-23

WANNA READ MORE?
Matthew 9:2-13
Mark 2:1-17

28.
JESUS BREAKS DUMB RULES

Here's how I checked the boxes:

Dear Kirby,

Do you like movies?   Yes **X** No ___

Do you like books?   Yes **X** No ___

Do you like ice cream?   Yes **X** No ___

Do you like dogs?   Yes **X** No ___

Sincerely,

Zuri-Claire

I sent the note back the same route it came. We're really communicating now.

Ahem.

Kirby here.

The grumpy religious leaders of Jesus' day loved rules, rules, and more rules!

Some rules were good, and some were dumb, but these grumps loved them all. They even added rules to their rules. All these extra rules complicated things and made it hard for people to follow God. And if you broke one of their rules, then "SHAME, SHAME, DOUBLE SHAME!"

The good rules were from God. Like—don't work on the Sabbath—that's one of God's Ten Commandments. The reason was so people could get a rest and worship God with joy. See, God always wraps his commandments in love. His commands *helped*, not *harmed* people. But the grumps took this good rule, added some extra stuff to it, and then used it like a big stick to bash people over the head.

A mysterious thing was happening in Jerusalem in those days. There was this swimming pool inside the city, and crowds of sick people lay poolside. Blind. Paralyzed. Lots of hurts. Every so often the pool bubbled up, and word on the street was that an angel had stirred it. The first person who jumped into the water after this happened would be healed.

CANNONBALL! ⟶

113

It became a big race. But a race isn't easy if you can't walk, right?! Or if you're blind and can't see bubbling water. So many folks who lay around that pool were not just hurting, but disappointed too. One dude had been sick for 38 long years!!! He couldn't walk, and you can imagine his frustration year after year as the water bubbled and someone with better legs made it in first.

Jesus walked by, saw the man, and said, "Hey, would you like to get well?"

"Can't do it," the man said. "No one helps me. Someone always gets into the water before me."

This deeply disappointed dude had given up hope. Wouldn't even try anymore. But Jesus had another plan.

"Stand up!" Jesus said. "Pick up your mat and walk!"

Instantly the man was healed. Wow—can you imagine the crowd gasping? A disabled man walking! He picked up his mat and flashed a big smile. Happy day!

But guess who wasn't happy.

Yep, the grumpy guys worried about keeping dumb religious rules. "Hey!" they yelled at the man. "It's the Sabbath. You just picked up your mat. Rules say no work—no picking up mats—and you just broke the rules. SHAME, SHAME, DOUBLE SHAME!!!!!" But "no picking up mats" wasn't a rule from God. It was a dumb rule they'd added to make life difficult.

Sheesh.

Another time, Jesus and his friends were walking through some grain fields. The disciples, always hungry dudes, broke off some heads of grain, shucked out the kernels, and chew, chew, chewed.

It was another Sabbath, and the grumpy religious rule-followers saw this and made a big stink. "Hey, you broke the rules again!!! Yeah. Picking grain is work. Neener-neener-boo-boo!!"

Jesus said, "Fellas, haven't you read in Scripture what King David did way back when?

He and his gang were on the run from despicable King Saul. They were hungry, so they ate the sacred bread only priests are supposed to eat—and they weren't condemned. Instead of bragging about keeping rules, you should think about how God is way more concerned about us being merciful to each other."

Another day, Jesus met a man whose hand was all messed up. This time the grumpy religious types wanted to trap Jesus. They sidled up to him and said, "Hey there, Jesus. Sabbath and all. What are you gonna do—hmmm?"

Jesus answered his critics with questions: "Is the Sabbath a day for doing good or doing evil? A day to save life or destroy it?"

But they wouldn't answer.

Jesus was ticked at the grumps and deeply saddened that they'd missed the whole point of what God was about.

Then Jesus said to the man, "Hold out your hand." Instantly it was healed.

But the grumpy guys left in a huff.

See, good rules are always needed—like stopping at a red light or obeying your parents. But people thought they could win God's favor by making up extra fiddle-faddle rules. That's just silly.

Jesus said, "Hey, wanna get right with God? Follow me, and learn what that means. I'm here to love you, not be hard on you. If you're tired and carrying a heavy burden, then come and I'll give you rest. Let me teach you how to live. I'm a gentle teacher, and when you follow me you learn to live freely."

Remember: Jesus broke dumb, grumpy-human rules that hurt people instead of helping them. Jesus

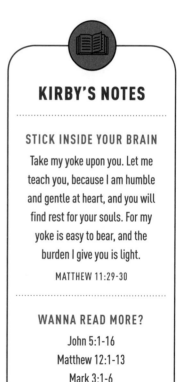

KIRBY'S NOTES

STICK INSIDE YOUR BRAIN

Take my yoke upon you. Let me teach you, because I am humble and gentle at heart, and you will find rest for your souls. For my yoke is easy to bear, and the burden I give you is light.

MATTHEW 11:29-30

WANNA READ MORE?

John 5:1-16
Matthew 12:1-13
Mark 3:1-6
Romans 10:4

fulfilled the good rules by accomplishing the greater purposes of God's law, always pointing people to himself and God's love and forgiveness.

Have a fantastic week, friends. Kirby has left the building.

29.
JESUS' SERMONS DON'T PUT YOU TO SLEEP

Guess what? Olivia is turning 11 and inviting EVERYBODY from junior church to a roller-skating party. Including me.

Including Zuri-Claire.

Get my drift? Wooooh! I'm so stinking excited!

Wait. Do I know how to roller-skate?

Ahem.

Jesus made lots of friends. Twelve followers became his closest pals: Simon Peter the Rock. James and John, the Sons of Thunder. Peter's brother Andrew. Philip. Nathanael (aka Bartholomew). Levi (aka Matthew). Thomas. James. Thaddaeus. Simon the Zealot. And Judas Iscariot, the flashiest of the bunch (actually, the group's treasurer who carried the cash).

Disciple trading cards—collect the original 12. (Can you spot Judas?)

Before Jesus got down to the business of saving us, he had things to teach these dudes—and us—about how to live. One day he hiked up a hill overlooking the Sea of Galilee, sat down, and began to teach the crowd that had followed him. The disciples gathered close.

What Jesus said that day became known as a pretty famous speech called the Sermon on the Mount. Just for kicks, give it a listen, and see how it applies to you. I promise: it won't put you to sleep.

Here's the gist of what Jesus said:

> God blesses you at the strangest times. Like when you're poor, hungry, or crying. He blesses you when folks don't like you or say nasty stuff about you because you belong to me.
>
> Then you realize how much you need God, and he comforts you and shows you mercy.
>
> When people make fun of you for following me, be happy. It's no fun to be mocked, but you're standing by me, and I'll give you a big reward in heaven.
>
> See, that's exactly where you should be—right out there with people who don't know me. Your job is to be like salt, keeping things tasty and clean, and like light, showing people the way to go.
>
> Remember, I've come to earth not to destroy the rules that Moses gave from God. I'm here to fulfill those commandments, pointing people to God's love and forgiveness.
>
> For instance, everybody knows "don't murder" is a law, right? And people do right when they don't murder anybody. But I want you to go further. Develop that law all the way to its full potential. Don't stop at "don't murder." Don't even call people names. Don't swear at people. That's the spirit of the law: let love guide your actions.

Keep your thoughts clean—another wise way to live. If something in your life makes you think about yucky stuff, then get rid of whatever's clogging your head. Clear the junk from your mind.

Don't take revenge. If someone's mean to you, don't be mean back. That's no way to live—them hurting you, you hurting them. It's a lot better to pray for bullies. Be like your Father, God, who loves everyone, good and bad.

When you do good stuff, don't do it just so people admire you. Some folks make a big splash out of giving to charity. But that's all the reward they'll ever get. You—just give quietly. God sees and will reward you.

When you pray, don't make a huge show. Big, fancy words aren't what God looks for. Just talk to God normally, naturally. Here's how to pray:

Hello, Father in heaven, your name is holy.

May your Kingdom come soon.

May everything you want to be done
*   today be done.*

Thanks for our food.

Please forgive our sins, just like we forgive
*   folks who do wrong to us.*

Help us to say NO WAY! to temptation.

Amen.

I wouldn't mess with the Sons of Thunder.

Lots of people run after money—why? Stuff you buy just gets rusty and moth eaten in the end. Instead, invest in the work of heaven—it lasts forever. Put your time, energy, and smarts there.

Don't worry about stuff. Food? Hey, God feeds the birds; he'll definitely feed you. Clothes? Hey, look at how God dresses up the wildflowers; he'll absolutely care for you.

Have a little faith. God already knows your needs. Make following God your first and most important goal, and he'll give you everything else you need.

Don't look down on people. Keep praying instead.

God is a good Father. Just think: if you ask your dad for a slice of toast, he won't give you a rock. If you ask for barbecued trout, he won't hand you boiled snake. God's a good, good Father, and he knows how to give good, good gifts.

Treat other people the way you want to be treated. (That's called the Golden Rule.)

The highway to hell is wide and fast—put your pedal to the metal and you'll get there quick. But the pathway to God's Kingdom isn't as obvious. Watch carefully—it's easy to miss.

In conclusion—follow my teaching and be wise, like the dude who built a house on solid rock. Another guy built on shifting sand, and when storms came, the house on sand fell down flat. The house on rock stayed firm.

↑
Philip wishes he had a nickname too. Phil? Philly? Phil the ditch with dirt?

When Jesus finished the Sermon on the Mount, the crowd was amazed. Jesus' teachings were the real deal.

We'll look at more amazing stuff about Jesus and how people began to line up for and against him.

Just remember: Jesus taught the truth.

Have a great week!

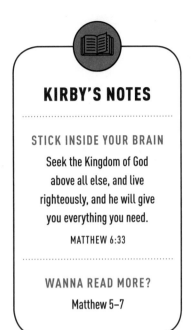

KIRBY'S NOTES

STICK INSIDE YOUR BRAIN

Seek the Kingdom of God above all else, and live righteously, and he will give you everything you need.

MATTHEW 6:33

WANNA READ MORE?

Matthew 5–7

30.
JESUS IS
THE BOSS

So, I know how to ride a skateboard. But I've never ever roller-skated. But they've gotta be sort of alike, don't you think? I mean, how hard can roller-skating be?

I asked the guys—Noah. Mason. Felipe. Jayden, Jo-Jo, even Jimmy. Everybody was like, "Yeah, sure. No problem."

But the last thing I want to do is to make a fool out of myself in front of everybody. Know what I mean?!?!?!

Only four weeks left until Olivia's party.

Ahem.

Hi there, savvy skaters.

After Jesus preached that corker of a good sermon, he went down the mountainside and headed for the town of Capernaum. Lots of people followed.

Remember, all the land of Israel was under Roman control in those days, and nobody liked the Roman soldiers very much, because they were the tough guys hired to enforce the iron will of Rome. But one day a Roman army officer cut through the crowds, came to Jesus, and pleaded, "Lord, my young servant is lying in bed, paralyzed, sick, in terrible pain, and near death."

"You want me to go to your house and heal him?" Jesus asked.

"Nope," said the army officer. "Lord, I'm not worthy to have you come into my home. Just say the word from where you are, and my servant will be healed long distance. I know this because I'm a man under the authority of officers of higher rank. And I have authority over soldiers with lower rank. If I say, 'Go,' then they go. If I say, 'Come,' then they come. I understand how authority works."

Jesus was impressed by the Roman's faith. "Go on back home," Jesus said to him. "Because you believed, it has happened." And guess what? The young servant was healed right at that moment.

Soon afterward, Jesus approached the village of Nain, with another large crowd following him. They met a funeral procession that was heading out of town. A young man had died, the only son of a widow, which was really tragic. The woman had lost her husband, and now she'd lost her son, too. In those days, there weren't a lot of jobs for widows, so that meant it was going to be really hard for the woman to get by. Besides that, she was now crazy lonely. Everybody was totally sad for her.

But Jesus said to the woman, "Don't cry." Then he walked over to the coffin and touched it, and the funeral procession screeched to a halt. "Dude!" he said to the dead young man. "You aren't dead anymore! Get up!"

And the dead boy got up, alive again. Wow, can you picture that? The boy was probably wrapped in graveclothes like a mummy. He probably pawed at the wrappings around his eyes and face and maybe sneezed a few times. I mean, this guy had been stone-cold dead, on his way to the graveyard. There was nothing anybody could do.

Except Jesus. He bossed death around. No funerals today! Nope! Not when Jesus says no.

I asked Grandpa McCook about this, and he said—uh—how exactly did you explain this, Grandpa?

KIRBY'S NOTES

STICK INSIDE YOUR BRAIN

God is so rich in mercy, and he loved us so much, that even though we were dead because of our sins, he gave us life when he raised Christ from the dead. (It is only by God's grace that you have been saved!)

EPHESIANS 2:4-5

WANNA READ MORE?

Matthew 8:5-13

Luke 7:11-17

The kids in the class all half turned to see what Grandpa would say, and he cleared his throat and smiled and said, "Well, this is what Jesus does for us today, too. Maybe he doesn't bring physically dead bodies back to life as a habit. But without Jesus, we're all spiritually dead in our sin. And being dead is a big problem. If you're dead, you can't do anything to help yourself. But through Jesus, the spiritually dead can be raised to life. That's the message of Jesus' good news. Jesus doesn't ask you to clean up your act by your own power. Jesus brings you back to life by his power! Our cold, clammy hearts start to beat again, thanks to God. Jesus gives us new life!"

Grandpa was getting pretty excited and waving his hands around to help us see this truth that is so wonderful to him.

And wow. It really makes Jesus the best superhero ever, right?

We'll check out more about that next week. See you then.

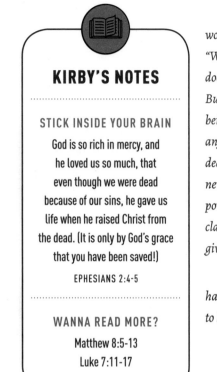

← It's the "Jesus gives us new life" dance.

31.
JESUS MAKES DEBTS VANISH— POOF

Don't ask Grandpa McCook about roller-skating if you want to know anything helpful. I asked him, and he started going on and on about some kind of steel-wheeled plates that you strapped to the bottom of your shoes and some sort of key thingy that adjusted them to your size.

I still don't have a plan.

Ahem.

We've been watching Jesus do all kinds of incredible miracles and bring dead people back to life, but he did ordinary stuff, too, like eat dinner. One day, one of those grumpy religious rule followers asked Jesus to have dinner with him, so Jesus went to the guy's home.

The meal probably started out the usual way with everybody catching up on news and whatnot. Then the evening kinda went nuts.

A woman who'd led a hard, sinful life had heard that Jesus was eating there, so she entered the house carrying a huge jar of really expensive perfume. She was genuinely sorry for the life she'd led, sorry for all the lousy things she'd done, and she knelt at Jesus' feet and just sobbed. Her tears fell on Jesus' feet, and she wiped them off with her hair.

She slathered the expensive perfume on Jesus' feet, and the delightful stink filled the whole house.

This was actually a pretty cool thing to do. But the host, the religious rule follower, saw this and had some grumpy thoughts: *Hoo boy, if Jesus knew who this lady was and all the junk she's done, I bet he wouldn't even let her touch him. She's bad, bad news!*

Jesus, always a mind reader, said to the host, "Hey, I've got a story to tell you."

"Okay," said the grumpy guy. "I love a good story."

Jesus said, "A man with stacks of money loaned cash to two guys. To the first guy, the man loaned 500 silver pieces. To the second, 50 pieces. Neither guy ended up being able to repay the loan, but the man was really nice, so he canceled both debts. They owed nothing. Zero. Zilch. Nada. So, question for you: Afterward, which of the two guys do you think was more grateful?"

The grumpy host answered, "The one who had the bigger debt canceled, I guess."

"Right you are," Jesus said. "Now think about this woman sitting here at my feet who came just to express her worship. Her many sins have been forgiven, and that's why she's doing this. A big debt's been canceled in her life. She's extremely grateful to God—that's what's happening here. Now let's compare her actions to yours, because your sins are

This guy should be happy too!

126

forgiven too, if you ask. When I entered your home, you didn't offer me water to wash the dust from my feet, but she went the extra mile and washed them with her tears. You didn't greet me with a friendly kiss on the cheek, as is the custom in these parts, but she's gone almost overboard, kissing my feet again and again. She's shown me much love. And that's a really good thing. How about you?"

Then Jesus said directly to the woman, "Your faith has saved you. Go in peace."

But some of the dudes around the table weren't happy with this.

An uneasy situation started brewing—can you feel it? Lots and lots of people liked Jesus—or at least they liked what he did for them. But a certain group of grumpy uptight people didn't like Jesus much at all—and their dislike of Jesus was growing and building and getting hotter and about ready to explode.

What could possibly go wrong with this situation? We'll explore this more soon.

For now, remember: Jesus is the boss. He bossed around the biggest enemy—death. So he's THE BOSS of all bosses. And as the Big Boss, he's the only one who can forgive our debts, that is, our sins, no matter how huge they are. By the way, have you asked him to cancel your debts?

Okay, cool kiddos, till next time. Kirby is out of here.

KIRBY'S NOTES

STICK INSIDE YOUR BRAIN

God saved you by his grace when you believed. And you can't take credit for this; it is a gift from God. Salvation is not a reward for the good things we have done, so none of us can boast about it.

EPHESIANS 2:8-9

WANNA READ MORE?

Luke 7:36-50
Ephesians 2:1-9

32.
JESUS LIKES FICTION

I searched "how to roller-skate" on the Internet, and I'm in big trouble.

Ahem.

Where were we? Oh yeah . . .

Jesus began a tour of nearby towns, telling the Good News about God's Kingdom. He took his 12 disciples along, plus a bunch of other follower dudes, plus some women who followed him—Mary Magdalene, Joanna, Susanna, and others.

Things were really heating up with the grumps who opposed Jesus. They accused Jesus of all sorts of rubbish, including being partners with the devil—a big stinking lie filled with rotten fish.

One day Jesus climbed into a boat and taught from there as a crowd on shore listened. He often told *parables*, fictional short stories designed to teach a lesson.

You know what *fiction* is, right? Like, in the library, all the books are either *non-fiction*—stuff that actually happened—or *fiction*—stories that are made up.

Some people swell up their chests and make a face like they've just eaten a lemon and announce, "Ugh. Fiction. I only read nonfiction, because I only like TRUE stories. I never read fiction, because it's made up—FALSE. I'm headed now to the Museum of Brainy

Intellectual Things to read nonfiction all day long—you go ahead and eat cookies and read novels."

That's crazy talk! Although fictional stories are made up, there's TRUTH in fiction too. The truth comes wrapped in a story. Jesus used fiction as a strategy to capture people's attention and present truth powerfully.

Here's one of my favorite fictional stories that Jesus told:

A farmer planted seeds, scattering them across his field. Then four things happened:

First, some seeds fell on a hard path, and birds gobbled them up. *Mmmph, chomp, gobble.*

Second, some seeds fell on rocky soil and sprouted quickly but soon withered under the hot sun. Since the roots weren't deep, the plants died. And there were many tears. *Boo-hooo.*

Third, some seeds fell among thorns that choked out the tender plants. *Aaagggghhh! Foot-stomping!*

Fourth, some seeds fell on rich soil and produced a huge crop. *YAY!!!*

"What's your story supposed to mean?" asked the disciples.

Jesus explained,

> Any person can be like a farmer by taking God's Word and "planting" it in others—telling them what God says. The seed on the footpath is a picture of people who hear the message, but the devil snatches it away. The seed on the rocky soil represents those who hear the message and respond joyfully, but without deep roots—habits of believing and obeying God. They don't last long. When hard times come, they stop following God. The seed among thorns represents people who hear God's Word, but soon life's worries crowd out the message. The seed on good soil represents those who hear and truly get God's Word.

"Oh, that makes sense," the disciples said.

I asked Grandpa McCook what this means for modern times, and he said, "Here's an example: you know how kids sometimes go to summer Bible camp and make decisions to follow Christ?"

"Sure," I said.

"Well, some of those decisions will stick, and others won't," he said. "The parable of the four soils helps explain why. When the going gets tough, some kids bail on faith. But the faith of other kids survives and thrives."

"Hmmm," I said. "How do you know if a person is truly following Jesus or not? If the kid made a decision to follow Christ at camp, is that all that's needed?"

"Yes and no," Grandpa McCook said. "People are saved by God's grace through faith when they put their trust in Jesus. So it's not hard to become a Christian in the first place. But if nothing more ever happens other than the initial decision, then you have to wonder if the person truly decided to follow Jesus or not."

"Wow," I said. "That's serious stuff. How can anyone know if they're really saved?"

Grandpa McCook showed me in the Bible—uh—where's that again?

"Got it right here," Grandpa said from his recliner. *"It's 1 John 5:11-13: '[God] has given us eternal life, and this life is in his Son. Whoever has the Son has life; whoever does not have God's Son does not have life. I have written this to you who believe in the name of the Son of God, SO THAT YOU MAY KNOW you have eternal life.'"*

Then he looked at me to carry on.

Gulp. Well, Grandpa McCook read that to me just last night after supper, and then looked me in the eye and said, "Okay. Do you or don't you have Jesus in your life? In other words, do you believe in Jesus?"

I nodded and said, "Yeah, I've got Jesus in my life. I believe in him. But how do I know for sure?"

He handed me the Bible and asked, "What does that verse say again?" He had me read it for myself. I got it. SO THAT YOU MAY KNOW! Duh. What a relief.

See you later, alligators.

KIRBY'S NOTES

STICK INSIDE YOUR BRAIN

He has given us eternal life, and this life is in his Son. Whoever has the Son has life; whoever does not have God's Son does not have life. I have written this to you who believe in the name of the Son of God, so that you may know you have eternal life.

1 JOHN 5:11-13

WANNA READ MORE?

Matthew 13:1-23

Luke 8:1-3

33.
JESUS TELLS THE BEST STORIES

I came in to junior church a couple minutes later than usual, and there was Jimmy sitting in Grandpa McCook's chair, working the lever that tilts it backward and forward and pops up the foot-rest. He stuffed his hands into all the side pockets and came up with a package of licorice, a notebook, a wrench, and a comic book.

"Wow," said Jimmy, "You could just live in this chair!"

I said, "Hey, birdbrain, what do you think you're doing?" and started working up a head of steam, but then Grandpa came in, and he just smiled.

"Yeah, it's a great chair," Grandpa said. "Anybody else want a turn?"

I had to interrupt Grandpa explaining the chair's mechanism to Jayden so we could get class started.

Ahem. Ahem!

Let's get cracking.

Remember, we were looking at some short stories—fiction—that Jesus told us to teach important truths. We'll see a couple more today.

Absolutely awesome pearl.
Never on sale.
Cost: EVERYTHING!

Jesus told this parable about God's Kingdom being like a mustard seed—a teeny-tiny seed. But you plant it, and what happens? *Bam!* It becomes a huge garden plant, growing long branches that birds can build nests in.

Jesus didn't always explain his stories—and he didn't explain this one. Grandpa McCook and I looked it up in an old book of his and found that mustard seeds can grow into plants anywhere from four to fifteen feet tall, and the plants grow bigger each year.

The point of the parable seems to be that small things can grow into really large things. Especially when it comes to spiritual matters. Maybe you think your faith is pretty teensy-weensy right now. Keep going. Keep following Jesus and getting to know him more and more. Keep reading your Bible and praying and hanging out with people who draw you toward Jesus.

Then just watch what happens.

Here's another parable Jesus told:

The Kingdom of Heaven is like a businessman on the lookout for the absolutely best pearls. Maybe he has all his secretaries and drivers and investors helping him look.

One day the man finds the *absolutely* best pearl he's ever seen, better even than the best of the *absolutely* top pearls. This pearl is *absolutely* amazing! He goes and sells *absolutely* everything else he's got, the things of lesser value, so he can buy the Pearl Worth Everything. That's a lot of *absolutelys*, but this pearl was ABSOLUTELY AWESOME.

Jesus didn't explain this parable either. I asked Grandpa McCook about it, and he said, "Well, there are two ways you can look at it. First, picture Jesus as the pearl, and we're like the businessman. There are plenty of beautiful things in this world. But one thing is more valuable than anything else—Jesus himself. It's not like you can buy him, but you want to be willing to trade everything else to follow him. Second, you could look at the story the other way around: picture Jesus as the businessman and us as the pearl. Just like the businessman is seeking valuables, God is always seeking lost sinners. God loves us so much that he was willing to go to extreme lengths to buy us from sin—God sent his Son to die on the cross for us, and that was an exorbitant cost! He gave a lot for us, because he loves us so much.

Wow, it's a neat story that can do a flip-flop and teach a lesson right side up or upside down.

All the time Jesus was telling these fun stories with important lessons tucked inside and people were relaxed and enjoying being with him and learning great stuff, Jesus' enemies got madder and madder, muttering about him working with Satan. Even some of his own family members worried that Jesus was having mental health issues.

But he kept on telling his stories. Jesus told many more parables than these, lots more than I can talk about in our junior church time. Jesus just used fun stories to build truth into the lives of his followers, a little more each day, because he knew that one day soon he'd need to go to the cross and do the work of being our Savior, the main work he came to earth to do.

For now, remember: Jesus used the technique of storytelling to teach truth, truth that helps us live the way he wants us to live.

Have a great week, you second-to-none squirts.

KIRBY'S NOTES

STICK INSIDE YOUR BRAIN

We are God's masterpiece. He has created us anew in Christ Jesus, so we can do the good things he planned for us long ago.

EPHESIANS 2:10

WANNA READ MORE?

Mark 4:30-34
Matthew 13:44-46
Mark 3:20-22

34.
JESUS DOESN'T FREAK OUT IN STORMS

Hoo man. Life is so incredible right now!!! Olivia had her party yesterday at the roller-skating rink, and all of us kids were there. We all got our skates and headed out onto the floor. It felt all crazy at first, a bit like skateboarding but completely different too. Most of us grabbed the walls and inched our way around the rink a few times.

Then I started getting the hang of it. I let go of the rails and was off and running. Er, skating. It wasn't pretty, but I was doing all right for my first time, if I do say so myself. In another half hour or so, I was getting smooth.

That's when the most incredible thing happened. The announcer at the skating rink stopped the fast, funky music and said, "Okay, we're going to have a couples skate. Everybody grab a partner and hold hands while you skate."

I just about fell over from shock. Jimmy, standing next to me, right then let out with another huge horse sneeze: AAAAA-CHOO-OO-OOOOOO!!!! All over both of his hands. Gross! Then he grabbed Olivia's hand, and I think she was about to barf, but she had the good manners just to smile and keep skating. So they were off.

That's when I felt a tap on my shoulder. Zuri-Claire was behind me. She'd been skating a few times before, I could tell, because she wasn't falling or wobbling. She sort of shrugged, and I sort of shrugged, and the announcer started this dreamy music, and just like that—Zuri-Claire and I were skating together HOLDING HANDS!!!!!!

I LOVE ROLLER-SKATING!

After that, we all ate pizza until we were cheesy and bloated. Then Olivia opened her gifts. We all skated some more. Except Jimmy, who's allergic to cheese and had another sneezing fit. (You gotta feel for the guy.) I hoped there'd be another couples skate, but no dice. Ah well, maybe next time.

Ahem.

Good morning, everybody. I hope you all brought a number two pencil. I'm not sure why, but it seems like something teachers are supposed to say, right?

Best. Day. Ever!

(I may still be a little off balance.)

Remember how Jesus was sitting in a boat and teaching people? Well, evening arrived, and the teaching was finished for the time being, so Jesus told his disciples to crank up the outboard motor and cross to the other side of the lake. Actually, they probably grabbed oars or hoisted the sail.

About halfway across, the wind picked up and the waves grew larger and pretty soon the disciples realized they had on their hands a FULL-FORCE GALE. I mean, we're talking the fiercest of fierce storms! Waves snarled and crashed over the side of the boat. The disciples grabbed buckets and tried to bail. But it was no use. The boat started filling with water. Everybody freaked out.

Except Jesus. He was at the back of the boat with his head on a cushion.

TAKING A NAP.

The disciples woke him up. They shouted, "HELP! SAVE US! WE'RE GOING TO DROWN!!!"

Jesus was never one to worry. I imagine he sort of yawned and stretched, took a look around, and said to the disciples, "Why are you guys so afraid? Have a little faith!"

Then Jesus told the wind and waves to knock it off. "PEACE! BE STILL," he said to the storm, and suddenly there was a great calm.

The disciples kept right on freaking out, but now for a different reason. They said, "Who is this man that even the wind and waves obey him?!?!" They could see he had to be somebody pretty incredible.

Wonder what Jesus would say to the things that scare us? That's something to think about till next week.

See you then, gang.

KIRBY'S NOTES

STICK INSIDE YOUR BRAIN

Don't worry about anything; instead, pray about everything. Tell God what you need, and thank him for all he has done. Then you will experience God's peace, which exceeds anything we can understand. His peace will guard your hearts and minds as you live in Christ Jesus.

PHILIPPIANS 4:6-7

WANNA READ MORE?

Matthew 8:23-27

Mark 4:35-41

Luke 8:22-25

35.
JESUS KNOCKS OUT BAD STUFF

I'm still hoping the party-arranger types will organize another skating party. I've dropped some hints, but I guess it's nobody's birthday anytime soon. Does it have to be? I'll keep hinting.

Ahem.

Fasten your seat belts. Here we go.

After the raging storm turned calm, morning dawned over the lake and probably looked swell. I wonder if the dudes in the boat thought about the fact that they had the Creator of Sunrises sitting right there in the boat with them.

When they got to shore, a bunch of people crowded around Jesus again, and a man named Jairus came and fell at Jesus' feet and asked Jesus to come home with him.

Jairus had a 12-year-old daughter, same age as me and some of you, and she was dying, which was a pretty serious problem. I can only imagine how scared and sad her dad felt. Jesus started walking to Jairus's home, and the crowd walked along with him.

Just then, a woman who'd been sick for 12 years came up behind Jesus and touched the hem of his robe. This woman had tried to get well for as many years as she'd been sick, and she'd spent a lot of money on the cures and had nothing to show for it except a clamshell of snake oil. No, not literal snake oil, Jimmy. It's an expression I learned from Grandpa McCook that means fake medicine. Anyway, nothing had ever worked. That is, until she met Jesus. The nanosecond she touched Jesus, the woman was healed.

"Who touched me?" Jesus asked.

"Everybody's touching you," Peter the Rock said. "You're walking along in a crowd, and they're all bumping into you."

"Nope," Jesus said. "One person deliberately touched me, and I felt healing power go out from me."

The woman began to tremble. She fell on her knees before Jesus and told her story.

"Go in peace," Jesus said. "Your faith has made you well."

Then everyone kept moving toward Jairus's house. But before they arrived, a messenger met them and said, "Don't bother. You're too late. The girl is dead."

Jairus probably felt like his world had just ended, but Jesus said to him, "Don't be afraid. Just have faith."

They reached Jairus's house, and Jesus took Peter the Rock and James and John, the Sons of Thunder, into the house with him. A crowd of people was there, and they were all weeping and wailing super loudly, as was the custom. "Why all the commotion?" Jesus asked. "The child isn't dead. She's only asleep." But the crowd laughed at him. They knew she was stone-cold dead.

Jesus, his three disciples, and the girl's mom and dad went into the girl's room. Jesus took hold of the child's hand and said, "Little girl, get up!"

And she did. Just like that. She stood up and walked around, and everybody in the room was totally amazed.

"Looks like she's hungry," Jesus said. "Give her something to eat."

Word of the miracle swept throughout the entire countryside.

After this, Jesus traveled through all the surrounding towns and villages, teaching folks about God. He healed lots of sick people, and whenever he saw the crowds, he had compassion on them.

"There's lots of spiritual work to be done," Jesus told his disciples, "but not a whole lot of workers to do it. Let's pray, asking God the Father to send more workers."

Okay, we're going to look at a really sad story next week. It doesn't have a happy ending, except that the guy went to heaven. We're not sure why some stories turn out that way.

For now, remember: lots of storms come into our lives. Sickness can feel like a storm. Death is a huge storm. But Jesus doesn't freak out in any kind of storm.

He's way bigger than any tornado or hurricane or tsunami. People who followed him around and paid attention this last while—they just had to have seen that Jesus was 100 percent God. He showed them that he is more powerful than nature or sickness or even death. If we're paying attention, we know that too.

And whatever gets thrown at us, we can stay calm. Trust in him. Have faith.

Have a great week, you admirable aces.

KIRBY'S NOTES

STICK INSIDE YOUR BRAIN

Let the peace that comes from Christ rule in your hearts. For as members of one body you are called to live in peace. And always be thankful. Let the message about Christ, in all its richness, fill your lives.

COLOSSIANS 3:15-16

WANNA READ MORE?

Matthew 9:18-26
Luke 8:40-56

36.
JESUS DOESN'T ALWAYS CHOOSE TO RESCUE

Jayden cornered me after junior church last week and asked, "What's with you and Zuri-Claire?"

EVERYTHING
YOU NEED TO KNOW WHEN YOU'RE 12

KIRBY McCOOK

"What is what with me and Zuri-Claire?" I replied.

"EVERYBODY says you're dating."

I almost choked. "Dating? We are not dating."

Jayden raised an eyebrow and said, "That's not what I heard."

Hoo man. I don't think I want to be dating. I'm not even sure if I'm allowed. Should I be dating? What do you do if you're dating? So many things to think about when you're 12. Somebody needs to write a book called Everything You Need to Know When You're 12. I bet it would make a gazillion dollars.

Ahem.

Okay, class, here's the sad story I told you we'd get to: things went from bad to worse for Jesus' cousin, John the Baptist.

Remember how John had been thrown into prison because he spoke out against Herod Antipas for kicking out his wife and marrying Herodias, his brother's wife? Herod didn't want to kill John because he worried it wouldn't be good politics. He knew that most people thought John the Baptist was a prophet. But Herod's safe plan for John was about to change.

On Herod's birthday, the king threw a big bash for his high officials and military commanders, all the leading dudes of his region. Picture a huge stone hall filled with greasy meat smells. Loud music. Dumb jokes. All sorts of shenanigans were going on. You get the drift.

In the middle of the party, Herod called for the dancing girls. Herod's niece/step-daughter, Salome, came out and danced for the men, and her act was a big hit.

"You can have anything!" Herod bawled to the girl when she finished. "I'll give it to you! Name it! Whatever you want, up to half my kingdom!"

Salome hesitated. Wow. Anything.

She went and asked her mother, Herodias, for advice, and Herodias saw her big chance to get even. Probably her eyes narrowed as she thought about it for a couple seconds and then hissed to her daughter, "Tell the king to bring you the head of John the Baptist on a serving dish."

Herod was in a real jam. He respected John and liked listening to him, although Herod often didn't understand what John was talking about. Sometimes he'd go down to the dungeon, pull up a stool, and get John talking about the Kingdom of God. He didn't believe that stuff, but he was curious, I guess. But because Herod had promised Salome anything she wanted, and he didn't want to look bad in front of the drunken men's club, he granted the request.

Out went the executioner, and in came John's head on a plate. Party over.

Well, John's disciples came for his body and buried it. Then they went and told Jesus what had happened, because when something troubling happens it's a good idea to tell Jesus. He was really sad and talked about how much he liked John and what great work John had done helping people get ready to meet the Savior.

So, yeah, Jesus could have jumped in and rescued his cousin from death, like he did for Jairus's daughter and others, but he didn't choose to do so. Sometimes Jesus lets evil continue, and bad things happen to good people. We don't completely know why, but here's what we do know:

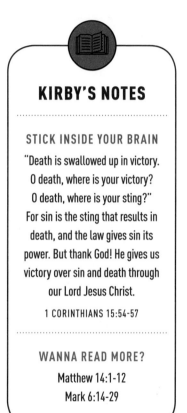

KIRBY'S NOTES

STICK INSIDE YOUR BRAIN

"Death is swallowed up in victory. O death, where is your victory? O death, where is your sting?" For sin is the sting that results in death, and the law gives sin its power. But thank God! He gives us victory over sin and death through our Lord Jesus Christ.

1 CORINTHIANS 15:54-57

- God is good, all the time, and he's powerful, all the time.
- Jesus would defeat death once and for all when he died on the cross.
- When a believer (like John the Baptist) doesn't get rescued and dies, he's immediately with God, and that's a far better place than anywhere on this old earth.

WANNA READ MORE?

Matthew 14:1-12
Mark 6:14-29

Chew on that this week.

37.
JESUS WHIPS UP LUNCH

Stories about lunch, like this one today, always make me hungry. I start thinking about my Mom's chocolate mousse. (That's not MOUSE, the rodent, but MOUSSE—sounds like moose. It's a kind of chocolate pudding that makes you think you're halfway to heaven.)

I wonder what Zuri-Claire's favorite food is? I can't believe I've never asked her! That would sure be an easy thing to talk about for a guy like me. Note to self: ask her what she'd like to eat if she was ever stranded on a desert island. As soon as you get up enough nerve to talk to her again!

Ahem.

I think you're really gonna like this story, because I've seen how you guys load up on burgers and fries.

It happened just after Jesus' disciples returned from a ministry tour, and Jesus planned to take them to a quiet place to regroup and rest. They jumped into a boat and headed to a secluded spot. But by now people recognized Jesus wherever he went, and a whole bunch of them ran along the beach and got there ahead of him.

Jesus sighed, took pity on the crowds, tied up the boat, walked up the hill a ways, and began to teach them. They kept asking for more. Late in the afternoon, his disciples came to him and said, "Uh, Jesus, we get it that you wanted to teach these folks instead of doing our retreat, but now it's getting late, and there aren't any restaurants around here. What are we all going to eat?"

"You feed the people," Jesus said.

"With what?" they asked. "We'd need to work for months and months to earn enough money to buy food for all these folks."

"How much food do we have on hand?" Jesus asked.

"We've got five loaves of bread and two fish," they said. "We, uh, borrowed those from a little boy. We don't know how happy he is about sharing his lunch with this huge crowd, but he said you can have it."

"Have the folks sit down," Jesus said. "It's time to feast."

He took the few loaves and fish, looked up toward heaven, and blessed the food. Then he started to break the meal up into pieces. He passed the pieces to the disciples who passed them to the people. And they just kept passing and passing and passing. Pretty soon everybody was like, "Wow, that Jesus can really stretch a meal!"

Sure enough, it was a miracle! They all ate as much as they wanted, and afterward the disciples picked up 12 baskets of leftovers. About 5,000 men were in the crowd, plus their wives and kids. That's probably 15,000 to 20,000 people total.

After the people ate their fill, they all kinda went nuts for Jesus. I mean—FREE FOOD, right?! They tried to make Jesus their king right then and there, but remember this: the Kingdom Jesus wanted was a spiritual kingdom of change in people's hearts, not a physical kingdom where he wore a crown and sat on a throne. So Jesus slipped away by himself into the hills to pray.

Jesus' disciples hightailed it out of there too. They got into their boat and headed out across the lake. Night fell, and another storm came up. A strong wind rose, and the disciples rowed hard, fighting heavy waves.

About three o'clock in the morning, after they'd rowed three or four miles, the disciples looked through the wind and rain and darkness and saw a figure walking toward them on the water. "Ga-ga-ga-GHOST!!!" they cried.

Right away Jesus called out, "Nope. Not a ghost! Don't be afraid. Take courage. I'm here."

Peter shouted, "Jesus, if that's really you, then let me walk to you on the water."

"Sure, come on over," Jesus said.

Peter hopped over the side of the boat and began walking on the water toward Jesus. But when Peter took his eyes off Jesus and looked around at the crashing waves, he became terrified and began to sink. "Help! Save me, Jesus!!!" Peter shouted.

Jesus reached out, grabbed him, and said, "Where's your faith, Peter? Why did you doubt me?"

They both climbed back into the boat. The wind stopped, and the disciples worshiped Jesus. "You really are the Son of God," they exclaimed.

When they docked, the crowd soon found Jesus, and he told them, "Here's the deal: you want to be with me because I fed you free bread, but that's not what's most important. What's important is this: I'm the Bread of Life. I sustain and nourish people. I'm the true Bread of Heaven that gives life to the world. Whoever comes to me will never be hungry again. Whoever believes in me will never be thirsty. Got that?"

Some of them did. Some didn't.

Okay, we'll see Jesus doing more miracles soon.

For now, remember: keep your eyes on Jesus.

Have a great week, you perfecto bambinos.

KIRBY'S NOTES

STICK INSIDE YOUR BRAIN

Jesus replied, "I am the bread of life. Whoever comes to me will never be hungry again. Whoever believes in me will never be thirsty."

JOHN 6:35

WANNA READ MORE?

Matthew 14:13-32
John 6:1-35

38.
JESUS SPITS

a very, very grossed-out Aisha

I gotta write Zuri-Claire another note. I really do.

Ahem.

Okay, everybody, listen hard.

This lesson is about a time when Jesus spit in someone's face. Well, not exactly. I mean, rude dudes do that if they're really ticked at someone, and it's a big insult, but that's not how it was at all.

Listen to the story: there was a blind man living in a town called Bethsaida. People brought him to Jesus and begged him to heal the man. Jesus took the blind man by the hand and led him outside the village. That's when things turned a little strange. Instead of just healing the man instantly, Jesus healed the man slowly, bit by bit. Here's how.

First, Jesus worked up a big loogie and spit on the man's eyes. No, I'm not kidding, Aisha. It's right there in the Bible. Then he laid his hands on the man's eyes. Yep. Crazy stuff maybe, but that's what Jesus chose to do, and

148

he always had good reasons. There was nothing insulting in this—it was an act of love by Jesus. Just wait and see what happens.

"How are things now?" Jesus asked.

"Well, I can see people, but I can't see them very clearly," the man said. "They look like trees walking around."

Jesus placed his hands on the man's eyes again, and this time the man's eyes were fully opened. His sight was completely restored, he saw everything clearly, and people didn't look like trees anymore.

Why? Why heal the man partway at first?

I talked this over with Grandpa McCook, and he said, first of all, don't look for anything magic in Jesus' saliva. His spit was just spit, like when *you* spit, your spit is just spit. He can use any old thing to accomplish his plan.

As to his plan for this man being a two-parter, there are at least two explanations—both right—because this is kind of a double picture.

First, it's a picture of how some people start to follow Jesus, but only halfway at the beginning. They aren't spiritually blind anymore—they're born again—but the eyes of their hearts are still cloudy. What these folks need is to allow Jesus to fully work in their lives and meet their needs. That's what Jesus wants, and it's what people who love these folks pray for.

Second, it's a picture of how Jesus knows exactly what people need. Sometimes people journey toward faith instead of slam-bam all at once coming to faith and being born again. It takes time for these folks to get it, to fully learn how to follow Jesus. So Jesus brings them along slowly, giving these people just what they need, when they need it. No sooner. No later.

After this, Jesus and his disciples traveled to an area called Caesarea Philippi, and he asked them, "Just curious: Who do people say I am?" Of course, Jesus knew everything. But he wanted to hear his disciples' answers.

They hemmed and hawed. "Well, some say you're John the Baptist. Others say you're

Elijah. Still others say you're Jeremiah or one of the other prophets." That's assuming any of those guys could come back from the dead, of course.

"Interesting," Jesus said. "But who do YOU say I am?"

Peter the Rock spoke first. "You are the Messiah, the Savior of the world, the Son of the living God."

Jesus said, "Nice going, Peter the Rock. One day you're going to help me out big-time by getting many people to believe just what you've said."

Then Jesus added to all the disciples, "You know, some hard times are coming. Lots of people will reject me, and I'm going to suffer some really hard things. I'll even be killed. But on the third day I'll come back to life."

A crowd had gathered around Jesus, and he turned to them and said, "It's not always easy to follow me, but if you truly want to, then you must set aside your own selfish plans. If you try to hang onto your life exactly how you expect it to go, then watch out—you lose. You lose out on the really great life God has planned for you."

Okay, countdown. We have liftoff. See you next week.

KIRBY'S NOTES

STICK INSIDE YOUR BRAIN
If any of you wants to be my follower, you must give up your own way, take up your cross daily, and follow me. . . . What do you benefit if you gain the whole world but are yourself lost or destroyed?

LUKE 9:23, 25

WANNA READ MORE?
Mark 8:22-29
Matthew 16:13-28

39.
JESUS PUTS THE MAG IN MAGNIFICENT

Or maybe Zuri-Claire will write me another note. Sheesh. So much to think about.

Ahem.

Time for class.

You could go right up to Jesus and ask him anything. Like this: one day a rich man came to Jesus and asked, "Good teacher, what do I need to do to get eternal life?"

"*Good*, huh," Jesus said. "Are you sure you know what you're talking about when you call me 'good'? Because only God is good. So only call me 'good' if you truly believe I'm God. But to answer your question—have you actually lived a perfect life? I know you think you have what it takes, but I know you inside and out."

"Sure," the rich man said. "I've been absolutely perfect since I was a kid. I don't steal. I don't lie. I haven't murdered anyone lately. God must be really pleased with me for being so perfect."

"Hmmm," Jesus said. "If you're actually trying to be perfect, here's what's lacking in your life. Go sell everything you have, give your money to the poor, then come and follow me."

The rich man's face dropped like an elevator with a cut cable. He went away sad, because he believed his money was super important, and he had lots to lose.

This camel is having none of that!

"Guys, it is super difficult for richer folks to get into God's Kingdom," Jesus told his disciples. "It can be harder than a big ol' humpbacked camel trying to squeeze through that teeny-tiny hole at the end of a sewing needle."

This really threw the disciples for a loop, because at that time a lot of people believed that if you were rich, it meant that God really liked you. "So who in the world can be saved?" they asked.

"If you're trying to get in good with God by being perfect, you're wasting your time," Jesus answered. "No one is perfect—and that's why you need the grace and mercy of God. Humanly speaking, it's impossible to be saved. But with God, everything is possible."

Another time, Jesus took his three closest disciples—Peter the Rock and James and John, the Sons of Thunder—on a hike up a mountain to pray.

As Jesus began to pray, an amazing thing happened. Picture the brightest light you've ever seen. Like the morning sun glittering on a river. Like the hottest welding torch—so bright you can't even look at it. Like the rays of a perfect sunset piercing the clouds. Jesus' face began to shine like that. Jesus was radiant. Ablaze. Glittering. Glorified. And his clothes shone a brilliant white.

Suddenly Jesus wasn't alone. Moses showed up, along with the prophet Elijah. They began talking with one another.

Peter the Rock, always practical, and not quite understanding what was happening, said, "Hey, this is pretty cool that all three of you are here. Why don't I put up three tents—and we can all stay for a while."

But even as Peter spoke, a bright cloud overshadowed them, and a voice from the cloud called out, "This is my dearly loved Son, who brings me great joy. Listen to him." The disciples shook in their boots and fell face-first, flat on the ground. They did the flop.

Then Jesus was alone. He came over to the disciples and said, "It's okay, guys. Get up. Don't be afraid."

When they hiked down the mountain, Jesus told them not to tell anyone about the experience until after he'd risen from the dead.

When I picture Jesus in my mind, I often think about that scene. I mean, sometimes kids talk about Jesus like he's any old buddy, just one of the gang. And it's true: Jesus is a friend in the sense that he draws close to people.

But Jesus definitely isn't any old pal. He's God, more radiant than any earthly king, clothed in brilliant, glorified splendor.

Like, how crazy would it be if I was on a hike with Jo-Jo, Jayden, and my dad—and suddenly my dad started glowing with a really white-hot radiance?! We'd all be like, whoa, what kind of crazy sunburn is this? I mean, that kind of transformation just doesn't happen to anyone. Ever.

That picture is what I like to remember when I think about Jesus. He's more glorious than any king on earth, more fantastic than any celebrity. In a word—Jesus is MAGNIFICENT.

Years later, when Peter the Rock was old, he wrote about this experience and said he was definitely not making this stuff up. He wrote, "We saw his majestic splendor with our own eyes when he received honor and glory from God the Father. We ourselves heard that voice from heaven when we were with him on the holy mountain."

Okay, some cool things definitely happened when Jesus was around. Healings. Teachings. Sights and sounds like never before. We're going to hear about more of these soon. For now, remember: Jesus is magnificent.

Have a great week, you unparalleled preteens.

KIRBY'S NOTES

STICK INSIDE YOUR BRAIN
We were not making up clever stories when we told you about the powerful coming of our Lord Jesus Christ. We saw his majestic splendor with our own eyes when he received honor and glory from God the Father. The voice from the majestic glory of God said to him, "This is my dearly loved Son, who brings me great joy." We ourselves heard that voice from heaven when we were with him on the holy mountain.

2 PETER 1:16-18

WANNA READ MORE?
Mark 9:2-13; 10:17-31
Matthew 17:1-9
Luke 9:28-36

40.
JESUS KNOWS THE ONE BIG THING

Who do you think should write the next note—me or Zuri-Claire?

Ahem.

Sisters Mary and Martha were close friends with Jesus. Personality-wise, Mary was a gentle soul, while Martha was a go-getter.

Jesus came to their house for supper, with all the disciples and their big appetites. Martha sprinted around the kitchen, stirring pots, adding spices, beating eggs, pounding dough. She worked herself into a tizzy. She had at least 13 hungry men on her hands, men who'd dropped in unexpectedly. What would you do? Make toast and open a can of beans? Nope, Martha had a reputation to maintain. So she cranked up the frenzy.

But Mary just sat at Jesus' feet listening to him.

The harder Martha worked, the more frustrated she became. So much work, and she was the only one doing anything!!! Finally, she burst from the kitchen. "Jesus, hey— would you PLEASE tell my sister to get cracking?! It's UNFAIR that Mary's just sitting there while I do all the work!!!"

Jesus said, "Martha, dear Martha, you're upset over all these details! There's only ONE THING worth being concerned about. Mary has discovered it."

What's that ONE THING? Sure, eating is important; people need to eat. But anxiety is a killer. So maybe Jesus was just telling Martha to chillax.

But it's much more. Grandpa McCook says the ONE THING probably referred to Psalm 27:4, where King David said that the ONE THING he asked of the LORD—the ONE THING he sought most—was to live in the house of the LORD, delighting in the LORD, and thinking thoughts of God.

That's what truly matters. Enjoying God.

In another story, Lazarus, the brother of Mary and Martha, got sick. I mean, the dude was really, really sick. The sisters sent for Jesus, and even though Jesus loved the family, he stayed put for two whole days.

Finally, Jesus told his disciples, "We need to go see Lazarus. He's dead."

"Dead? What do you mean dead?" asked the disciples.

"Well, he's *dead*-dead. How clear can I be?" Jesus said. "But you're about to see something really cool. C'mon."

Yep, Lazarus was truly dead. He had already been buried, and the mourners were wailing and weeping. When Martha heard Jesus had come, she went out to meet him.

"Jesus, if only you'd been here, my brother wouldn't have died," Martha said.

"Don't worry. Your brother is going to rise again," Jesus said.

"Sure, he'll rise again one day at the resurrection," Martha said.

"That too," Jesus said. "But guess what—I AM THE RESURRECTION and the life. Anyone who believes in me will live, both before and after dying."

Martha went and told Mary that Jesus was there and wanted to see her. Mary ran up to Jesus, sobbing, and said the same thing: "Jesus, if only you'd been here, my brother wouldn't have died."

Jesus asked, "Where have you put him?"

They took Jesus to Lazarus's tomb. For Jesus, the sight of that grave brought to mind how much he hated death. He got angry. Then he cried. Yep, he couldn't hold back the tears. Then Jesus walked straight to the tomb and said, "Roll the stone away!"

Martha said, "No way. By now he's been dead for four days. He'll stink!"

Jesus said, "Didn't I tell you that you'd see God's glory if you believe?"

So they rolled the stone away.

Jesus prayed, then shouted: "LAZARUS! COME OUT!"

And out came Lazarus, wrapped in graveclothes, blinking at the sunlight, fully alive.

"Unwrap him," Jesus said. "Death's done here."

Jesus and his disciples left for a while, but later they returned for a dinner in Jesus' honor. Martha served, and Lazarus and the others ate their fill of Martha's delicious meal. But Mary had other plans for the evening.

She took a 12-ounce jar of extremely expensive perfume and dumped it over Jesus' feet. Then she wiped his feet with her hair, and the fragrance of the perfume filled the house. It was a beautiful act of worship. Mary's an example of the people who had lined up on Jesus' side and were growing in love for him.

Does this make Lazarus a zombie?

But one of the disciples, Judas Iscariot, sneered and said, "What a waste! That perfume was worth a whole year's salary. She should have sold it and given the money to the poor!" Not that Judas cared so much about the poor—he was in charge of the disciples' money and often helped himself. He's an example of the people who lined up against Jesus and were growing in hatred for him.

"Leave her alone," Jesus told Judas. "You'll always find poor people anywhere. But you won't always have me with you. Mary did this in preparation for my burial."

The gloomy, uptight religious leaders heard about this, and about Lazarus being raised from the dead, and they were GRUMP-EEE. People flocked to hear Jesus, and the leaders didn't like this either. Their hatred of Jesus had built and built and was ready to burst, so they began to plot how to kill Jesus.

The dastardly deeds of these religious leaders and their henchmen are coming up fast in the story.

Remember: Jesus knew the ONE BIG THING that truly mattered—loving God.

Have a great week, you sterling sprouts.

KIRBY'S NOTES

STICK INSIDE YOUR BRAIN

The one thing I ask of the LORD—the thing I seek most—is to live in the house of the LORD all the days of my life, delighting in the LORD's perfections and meditating in his Temple.

PSALM 27:4

WANNA READ MORE?

Luke 10:38-42
John 11:1-44; 12:1-11

41.
JESUS SAYS: LOVE LOOKS LIKE THIS

I should definitely write Zuri-Claire a note first this time. I gotta find out if we're dating or not. Because if we ARE dating, I don't know what to do about it.

Ahem.

One day, a teacher asked Jesus, "What should I do to get eternal life?"

Jesus answered, "You teach the law. You tell me."

The teacher answered, "The law says we should love God and our neighbor."

"Right you are!" Jesus said. "Do that and you will live."

The guy wanted to feel good about how he was already living, so he asked, "And who is my neighbor?"

In response, Jesus told him a story.

A Jewish man traveled from Jerusalem to Jericho. Robbers roughed him up really bad. The man lay beside the road, bloody and bruised, and a bunch of folks who should have known better passed right by him.

But then a Samaritan (remember—Samaritans and Jews didn't usually get along) saw him and stopped. The Samaritan put the beat-up dude on his donkey, took him to an inn to be cared for, and paid his bills.

"That's what love looks like," Jesus said.

Another day, Jesus taught his disciples how to pray. You'd think they'd be naturals—I mean, they were already daily talking with God the Son. But Jesus used another story to teach them more.

Suppose you go to your buddy's house at midnight to borrow three loaves of bread.

(You couldn't just run to the corner store back then.)

You bang on the door and call, "A friend just arrived for a visit, and I have nothing for him to eat."

(Don't you love it when hungry friends arrive at midnight?!)

Suppose your buddy calls back, "Don't bother me. Everyone's in bed." But you keep knocking and knocking. Finally, your friend gets up to help.

"That's what prayer is like," Jesus said. "Keep asking, and you'll receive. Keep seeking, and you'll find. Keep knocking, and the door will be opened to you."

Another time, Jesus taught about how God shows his love by guiding and protecting people. He said, "Think of me as a Good Shepherd. My sheep recognize my voice, and I call them by name and lead them places and even sacrifice my life for them. The thief tries to steal the sheep, to hurt, kill, and destroy them. But my purpose is to give people a full and abundant life."

One day, James and John, the Sons of Thunder, came up to Jesus and said, "Hey, Jesus, we want you to do for us WHATEVER WE ASK."

Okay, stop. Picture yourself saying that to people in your life. Maybe your teacher at school. "Hey, Mr. Butterworth, Jimmy and I want you to do for us WHATEVER WE ASK!" Yeah, right. Your parents? "Hey there, Mom and Dad, me and Aggy and Jo-Jo want you to do for us WHATEVER WE ASK!" How crazy is that?! But that was the audacious question these dudes asked Jesus. Ridiculous.

Jesus took it in stride. He must have chuckled before he said, "Okay. What do you want me to do for you?"

James and John laid it out: "One day when you rule everything, we want to occupy the main places of honor. James sitting on your right, John on your left. Or vice versa; we're flexible. Pretty please with cheese?"

Jesus answered, "You don't really know what you're asking. Because if you truly follow me wherever, there'll be suffering. Are you able to do that along with me too?"

"Oh sure," they bragged. "No problem-o."

Then Jesus said, "I know the future, and hard times are coming for you both. But God the Father will decide who gets the most honored places in the Kingdom. So that's that."

When the other disciples heard about this, they were ticked at James and John. Probably because they wished they'd said the same audacious thing to Jesus first.

So Jesus called them together and said, "Hey, look. Everybody always wants to be number one, right? But when you follow me, you need to look at

Emma's having a hard time getting her mom to do WHATEVER SHE ASKED.

things differently. If you want to be a leader, then you need to serve others. That's how it goes in the Kingdom of God. That's what I'm all about. Pretty soon, I'm going to give my life away so others can truly live. That's supremely what love looks like."

Chew on that till next time. Kirby, over and out.

KIRBY'S NOTES

STICK INSIDE YOUR BRAIN

The most important commandment is this: "Listen, O Israel! The LORD our God is the one and only LORD. And you must love the LORD your God with all your heart, all your soul, all your mind, and all your strength." The second is equally important: "Love your neighbor as yourself." No other commandment is greater than these.

MARK 12:29-31

WANNA READ MORE?

Luke 10:25-37; 11:5-13
John 10:1-11
Mark 10:35-45

42.
JESUS LOVES YOU, DUDE

"Jimmy and Jo-Jo say they have a song for us today," I announced dubiously.

The two of them marched to the front, struck a pose with their air guitars, and belted out, "Baby slug inside the zoo! Wants outside—what will he do? In the air he feels a breeze. Tries to jump but has no knees. Baby slug inside the zoo—oo—oo!" They fell over each other and collapsed on the floor laughing, while everyone in the class groaned.

Ahem.

Okay, settle down. Actually, our lesson today is about people who need to be loved and some who seriously don't have anyone around to love them.

A bunch of parents brought their kids to Jesus for him to bless. But the disciples were in a bad mood that day and said, "Stop bothering Jesus. Can't you see he's busy? Get those snot-nosed brats out of here." Like a lot of grown-ups, their reaction to kids was basically, "Go away."

But Jesus heard this and said, "Knock it off, disciples. Let those kids come and see me." Jesus hugged all the kids and blessed them. Then he said to the disciples, "See these kids? That's what the Kingdom of God is like. They're smiling. They're trusting. They're depending. Their hearts are wide open to goodness. And that's just how a person needs to enter the Kingdom of God—with the attitude of a child, without all the complications of being an uptight, gloomy religious dude."

After that, some gloomy religious dudes came to Jesus and chewed him out, because he still hung out with slimeball tax collectors and other sinners, making sure they knew they were loved.

Jesus told them a story: "If a shepherd had a hundred sheep and lost one, don't you think he'd look for it? And if a woman had ten valuable coins and lost one in her house, don't you think she'd sweep every inch of her floor until she found it?

"That's what God is like with sinners," Jesus added. Then he told another story:

A good father had two sons. The younger son got greedy and told his dad to drop dead and give him his inheritance now—long before the father died. The father allowed the son to make bad choices, and the kid ran away to the ancient version of Las Vegas and blew all his money on wild living.

When the kid was broke, all his so-called friends left, and he had nobody at all. Then a famine hit the land. The kid got the only job he could find—feeding swine in a pigpen—and the job paid so lousy, and he grew so hungry that he actually eyed the pig slop and almost ate it.

Finally, he came to his senses, and said, "Man, I had it so good when I lived at home. Even my father's servants have food to spare. I'll go home, apologize to Dad, and tell him I've sinned against God and I'm no longer worthy even to be called a son. Maybe Dad will let me become one of his hired hands and work on his farm."

So the kid returned home. And here's the cool thing—while the boy was still a long way off, the father saw him coming and raced down the road, straight to his son, and gave him a huge hug. The father was filled with love and compassion for the boy and threw him a big homecoming party, which his older brother didn't like much.

"Rotten turnips!" said the older brother to his dad. "Why didn't you ever throw me a big party? I've always kept my nose clean."

"Son," the father said, "don't you know everything of mine is already yours? But we're celebrating because your brother was dead and now he's come back to life. He was lost, and now he's found."

Grandpa McCook told me that's how God the Father operates with people who are far from him. He's always watching down the road, waiting for them to come home. And when they do, it's party time.

But the gloomy teachers didn't like these stories one bit. They didn't like that Jesus called himself God, and that lots of people were following Jesus. Their anger grew and grew and grew—and was just about ready to explode.

For now, remember: Jesus is all about love. He guides people in love, he loves when we talk to him, he loves when we love others, and he loves when people far from him get close. Jesus loves everybody.

Okay, have a great week, you world-class whippersnappers.

KIRBY'S NOTES

STICK INSIDE YOUR BRAIN

God showed how much he loved us by sending his one and only Son into the world so that we might have eternal life through him. This is real love—not that we loved God, but that he loved us and sent his Son as a sacrifice to take away our sins.

1 JOHN 4:9-10

WANNA READ MORE?
Luke 15:1-32
Mark 10:13-16

43.
JESUS RIDES ONE LUCKY DONKEY

I wrote Zuri-Claire this note:

I gave it to Emma, who gave it to Olivia, who gave it to . . . you know how the mail chain works.

Ahem.

Heading toward Jerusalem, Jesus reached a village between Galilee and Samaria. Remember leprosy? Well, ten men with leprosy stood off a way, bawling, "Jesus, Master, have mercy on us!"

They were likely all disfigured and everyone thought they were gross, but Jesus didn't miss a beat. "Go show yourselves to the priests," he said. "You're healed."

All ten romped away, whooping and hollering. They were healed! But one man stopped, turned, and came back, shouting, "PRAISE GOD!!!" He fell at Jesus' feet and thanked him. He was a Samaritan, and you remember how folks felt about Samaritans?

"Hmm, just curious," Jesus said. "Didn't I heal ten men? Where are the other nine? Has no one returned to give glory to God except this foreigner?" Jesus smiled and said to him, "Stand up and go. Your faith has healed you."

Then Jesus told another story:

> Two men went to the Temple to pray. One was totally self-righteous. Thought he was perfect. The other guy was a slimeball tax collector. Everybody hated him.
>
> The self-righteous dude stood tall and prayed loud and proud so everybody could hear: "Oh God, I'm so happy I'm not like others—cheaters, sinners, slimeballs." He glanced at the tax collector and added with a sniff, "I do everything right. God, you sure must be happy to have me as your humble (*cough*) servant."
>
> The slimeball tax collector stood at a distance and looked at the ground. He beat his chest in sorrow and mumbled, "Oh God, please be merciful to me, for I'm a slimeball. I know I've done wrong. I'm so sorry. I desperately need you."

Jesus said, "Guess what? The tax collector, not the self-righteous dude, was celebrated by God. Those who lift themselves up all prideful will be humbled, yet those who humble themselves will be exalted."

In Jericho, on the way to Jerusalem, lived a short guy. (I'm sure he'd heard all the short-guy jokes.) He was Zacchaeus, the chief slimeball in the region. Yep, head tax collector, and loaded with cash. Zacchaeus heard Jesus was coming to town, and he wanted a good look, but he was too short to see over the crowd. So he ran ahead and shinnied up a sycamore tree.

I wonder if Jesus called him Zach.

When Jesus came to the tree, he stopped, looked up, and called the guy by name. "Zacchaeus! Come down. I'm going to be a guest in your house today."

(Jesus wasn't rude to invite himself. People didn't normally invite themselves to other people's houses back then, but nobody—I mean nobody—would be pals with a tax collector, much less eat at his house. So Jesus was actually honoring Zacchaeus, showing him grace.)

Old Zacchaeus quickly slid down the tree. With a big, genuine grin, he escorted Jesus home. And right then and there, Zacchaeus had a change of heart. "Lord, I'm truly sorry," he said. "I'm going to give half my wealth to the poor and return four times the stolen money to anyone I ever cheated."

Jesus said, "Nicely done, dude. Your action shows that salvation has come to your house today."

On Jerusalem's outskirts, something really cool happened. Jesus sent two disciples ahead to find a young donkey tied up—a colt, never ridden before. Jesus said, "Go ahead, untie it and bring it here. If anyone asks about it, just say, 'The Lord needs it.'"

Sure enough, the disciples found the colt, threw their coats on it like a saddle, and brought it to Jesus, who rode the donkey on into the city. The crowds turned the last bit of the trip into a huge, cool parade. They spread coats on the road before Jesus.

They cut leafy palm branches to lay before him, like a fancy red carpet—except it was green. As Jesus rode along, the crowds shouted and sang, praising God for all the miracles. I don't know the tune, but they sang these words:

> Blessings on the King who comes in the name of the LORD!
> Peace in heaven, and glory in highest heaven!

The song was from Psalms, and the gloomy religious leaders were like "Wait a minute. You can't sing that about Jesus. Hey, Jesus! Tell your followers to be quiet!" They knew those words were about the expected King-Savior-Messiah.

But Jesus said, "Nope. It's a day for praising God. If my disciples keep quiet, then the rocks and stones along the road will burst into songs." This was another fulfilled prophecy, the perfect time for a huge party.

But as Jesus got closer to Jerusalem, he grew sad, and even shed a few tears. He said, "How I wish today that all of you would understand the way to peace."

Hoo boy—now the grumpy-gus leaders got deadly serious about plotting to kill Jesus. We'll soon see how their plans played out.

Just remember: Jesus is worthy to be celebrated.

KIRBY'S NOTES

STICK INSIDE YOUR BRAIN

Rejoice, O people of Zion! Shout in triumph, O people of Jerusalem! Look, your king is coming to you. He is righteous and victorious, yet he is humble, riding on a donkey—riding on a donkey's colt.

ZECHARIAH 9:9

WANNA READ MORE?

Luke 17:11-19; 18:9-14; 19:1-9, 28-42
John 11:55-57; 12:12-18

44.
JESUS WASHES STINKY FEET

Zuri-Claire has not written back yet.

Ahem.

Before anything really bad happened to Jesus, he taught some more things we need to know. He told this story:

> A man went on a long trip. Before he left, he gave his three servants some money to use wisely while he was gone. To the first servant, he gave five bags of silver. The second got two bags. The third, one. Then the man left.
>
> The dude with five bags invested it wisely and earned five more. The servant with two bags also worked smart and earned two more. But the dude with one bag was a flake. He dug a hole in the ground and hid the money. Boo-ooo!
>
> The man came home and asked the servants how it went. They told him. The man praised the first two, saying to each, "Well done, my good and faithful servant." But to the third he said, "You really blew it. You could've at least put my money into the bank to earn interest. You're fired!"

Grandpa McCook explained that this story shows how we've all been given talents and abilities by God. Whoever uses them for God's work will be rewarded. But if you just waste what God gave you, well, you lose.

One day, Jesus and his disciples were sitting near the Temple collection box, watching people drop in their money. Rich person after rich person came by and dropped in big amounts. Then came one little old lady, a widow. She was so poor, she had only two pennies. She gave them both to God.

Jesus said, "That woman there—she gave more than anyone else. The guys who gave a lot of money only gave a fraction of their stash. But the widow gave all the money she owned."

This is awesome-possum sauce, right? Learning about Jesus, hearing his stories, and having fun getting to know him more. But the next few stories aren't fun at all. They're powerful. They're serious. They change everything. But they aren't fun. Just so you know.

Things started getting really bad with Judas. Remember him? He got greedy, went to the gloomy religious leaders, and said, "I can tell you where Jesus hangs out, in case you guys want to catch him. How much will you pay me to betray Jesus to you?"

"Thirty pieces of silver," they said.

"Yippee!" Judas said. "I'm rich!" So Judas started looking for his chance.

Meanwhile, the Jewish Passover holidays arrived, and Jesus invited his disciples to supper in an upper room. They all kind of laid on couches around a table, as people did in those days. But Jesus got up, took off his outer robe, wrapped a towel around his waist, and poured water into a basin. Then Jesus began to wash the disciples' feet, dusty and sweaty and smelly from walking around all day in sandals.

This shocked the disciples. Usually only servants did this. When Jesus got to Peter the Rock, Peter said, "No way. You're never going to wash my stinky feet."

Jesus said, "Unless I wash your feet, you won't belong to me." In other words, Jesus must serve us, and we must let him serve us and give us grace and forgiveness.

After washing the disciples' feet, Jesus put on his robe and said, "Do you understand what I just did? Since I'm your teacher and I washed your feet, you should wash each other's feet." In other words, serve one another in love.

They began to eat, and Jesus, now troubled, said, "Hey, I hate to say this, but one of you is going to betray me."

All the disciples were like, "One of us? No, never. Who?"

John, one of the Sons of Thunder, was next to Jesus. Peter the Rock leaned over to John and said, "Who's he talking about?" John whispered to Jesus, "Who is it?"

Jesus said, "I'm going to dip some bread into a bowl and give it to someone. That one is the betrayer." Jesus dipped bread in the bowl.

Judas said, "Teacher, am I the one?"

Jesus said, "Yep," and gave the bread to Judas, who ate it. Maybe John didn't see or hear this, or he was so shocked that he froze, because he didn't try to stop Judas. Jesus whispered, "Now hurry up and do what you're going to do." And Judas left the supper.

Sad, sad, sad, all the way to horrible. Let's hang onto that picture of Jesus washing our feet.

See you next week.

KIRBY'S NOTES

STICK INSIDE YOUR BRAIN

You have been called to live in freedom. . . . Use your freedom to serve one another in love.

GALATIANS 5:13

WANNA READ MORE?

Matthew 25:14-30

Mark 12:41-44

John 13:1-30

45.
JESUS FACES
THE WORST

Still no note from Zuri-Claire—maybe she's lost interest in me. But I've started to think lately that my troubles are pretty small ones, compared to some. Like—compared to Jesus and what he went through on this earth.

Ahem.

Let's continue the story of those last days of Jesus' life. Remember, he and the disciples—now minus Judas—were eating their last meal together.

Jesus said, "The time has come for God to glorify me. I'm not going to be with you much longer. So I want you to know for certain that you are supposed to love one another."

Peter the Rock said, "Where are you going? I want to go too."

"Sorry," Jesus said, "you can't come with me where I'm going."

"But I'll go anywhere with you," Peter said. "I'd go to jail. I'd even die for you."

Jesus smiled gently and said, "Really, Peter? Truth is, before this very night is over you're going to tell people you don't even know me. You'll do it not once, but three times. When the rooster crows early tomorrow morning, you'll remember what I said and you'll know, yup, you did it just like I'm saying."

"No way!" Peter said. "I'd never deny you." And all the other guys nodded and said, "No way! We're sticking with you. Uh-huh."

Jesus knew better, but he didn't argue. He told them, "Here's some good news. I'm not going to abandon you. God the Holy Spirit will be with you. He'll teach you the truth."

Then Jesus took a loaf of bread, blessed it, and broke it into pieces. He gave a piece to each disciple and said, "Take this and eat it, for it's a picture of my body broken for you." Then he took a cup of wine, thanked God, and said, "Each of you drink from it, for this is a picture of my blood, which is poured out as a sacrifice to forgive the sins of many."

They sang a praise song together, and then the Last Supper was over.

That evening, Jesus and his friends crossed the Kidron Valley and entered an olive grove called Gethsemane. He told the main group of disciples to sit and wait while he went to pray. Then he took Peter the Rock and James and John, the Sons of Thunder, farther into the garden.

"My soul is crushed with grief because of what's going to happen next," Jesus said. "Stay here and pray with me."

He went off a little distance and talked to God the Father. "Daddy," he said. "If it's possible, please don't let me suffer this horror that I'm facing. But what's important to me is whatever's important to you."

He came back to his disciples and found them all asleep. "Please wake up, friends," Jesus said. "Keep watch with me and pray."

Jesus went a second time to pray. "Daddy, Father," he said. "Please don't have me go through this agony that's coming next." He prayed so intensely that his sweat fell to the ground like drops of blood.

He went back to his disciples, and sure enough, they were all asleep again, so he went to pray a third time, and when he came back, they were still asleep.

"The time has come," Jesus said. And he woke them up and added, "Look, my betrayer is here."

We'll stop there, but I think you can guess the name of that betrayer.

For now, remember: Jesus would go through anything for us, and he did.

KIRBY'S NOTES

STICK INSIDE YOUR BRAIN

"Abba, Father," he cried out, "everything is possible for you. Please take this cup of suffering away from me. Yet I want your will to be done, not mine."

MARK 14:36

WANNA READ MORE?

1 Corinthians 11:23-26
Matthew 26:26-46
John 13:31-38

46.
JESUS DIDN'T DO IT

Zuri-Claire STILL HAS NOT WRITTEN BACK. But I can't think about that right now. Not with today's lesson.

Hey, kool kats.

We left off last week with the betrayer, Judas, heading toward Jesus with a crowd of rough tough men armed with swords and spears and holding blazing torches.

"Who are you looking for?" Jesus called. (He already knew.)

"Jesus of Nazareth," they called back.

Judas the Traitor slunk up close and kissed Jesus on the cheek. (This was the signal that Judas and the thugs had worked out beforehand, so they'd know the correct guy to arrest.)

"Greetings, Teacher," Judas said, all smug like a cockroach.

The henchmen grabbed Jesus and arrested him. But Peter the Rock pulled out a sword and slashed it around. He struck the high priest's slave, cutting off the man's right ear.

YUCK! ↗

Jesus said, "No more of this," and he touched the man's ear and healed him.

Then Jesus spoke to the men who'd come to arrest him, saying, "Seriously? Am I really that dangerous? You saw me tons of times in broad daylight teaching people at the Temple. Why didn't you arrest me then?"

Just then, the disciples realized they were sunk. They all ran for their lives. One young fellow wore only a long shirt, a tunic. He started running, and a burly dude grabbed the back of his shirt. Desperate, the young man slipped out of his shirt and ran away naked. "Aaaaauuugh! Gotta go!"

The thugs who'd arrested Jesus took him to the house of Caiaphas, the high priest, and all the gloomy religious leaders gathered around. Meanwhile, Peter followed at a distance into the courtyard, where a fire had been lit and people were crowded around it, warming up. Peter was feeling kinda chilly, so he went to the fire and warmed himself, too.

A servant girl noticed Peter the Rock. She said, "Hey—this guy follows Jesus."

"No I don't," Peter said.

"Yes you do," said someone else. "You must be one of them. A disciple."

"No way!" Peter said.

About an hour later someone else said, "You are too a follower of Jesus."

But Peter said, "No way, nohow. I don't even know this dude Jesus!" Right then, while he was still talking, the rooster crowed—just like Jesus had said. Peter realized he'd denied Jesus three times. He stumbled out of the courtyard, weeping bitterly, just sobbing his heart out.

The high priest drilled Jesus and accused him of saying that he was God. Jesus calmly answered that he was indeed who the high priest said he was. A guard slapped Jesus across the face. Then a bunch of guards spit in Jesus' face and beat him with their fists. Then they carted Jesus away to the Roman governor, a guy named Pilate.

Early that morning, Judas the Traitor realized what he'd done. He was stricken with remorse and tried to give back the thirty pieces of silver to the uptight religious leaders, saying, "Jesus was innocent! He didn't deserve any of this."

"What do we care?" they said. "That's your problem, not ours."

Then Judas threw the silver at them and went out and killed himself. A tragic end to Judas's life.

Meanwhile, Jesus was hauled before Pilate.

"Are you the king of the Jews?" Pilate asked Jesus.

Jesus answered, "My Kingdom is not an earthly kingdom."

Pilate went to the crowd that had gathered and said, "He's not guilty of any crime. He's from Galilee, isn't he? Herod Antipas is in charge of Galilee. Send him to Herod."

Herod happened to be in Jerusalem, so they dragged Jesus over to Herod, who asked Jesus question after question, but Jesus refused to answer. Herod finally gave up and just started mocking Jesus. His soldiers joined in. They put a royal robe on him and called him a bunch of bad names and sent him back to Pilate.

Pilate was still bewildered as to why so many people hated Jesus. "This man has done nothing that deserves the death penalty," he told the crowd. "How about this: I'll have him flogged, then release him."

"NO WAY!" shouted the crowd.

Then Pilate got a bright idea. He said, "Look—each year it's traditional to release a prisoner. I could give you Jesus, or uh, that other guy—what's his name?—yeah, Barabbas, the notorious murderer, a truly rotten guy. Of course, you'll choose Jesus, right?"

"BARABBAS!" yelled the crowd. "GIVE US THE BAD GUY, AND PUT THE INNOCENT MAN TO DEATH INSTEAD." Mixed up, big-time.

Pilate saw that they'd gone nuts, so he sent for a bowl of water and washed his hands before the crowd (as if water could wash away his guilt) and said, "I'm innocent of this man's blood. The responsibility is yours!"

"NO PROBLEM!" the crowd yelled back.

So Pilate shrugged, ordered Jesus to be whipped, then turned him over to Roman soldiers to be crucified.

KIRBY'S NOTES

STICK INSIDE YOUR BRAIN

God made Christ, who never sinned, to be the offering for our sin, so that we could be made right with God through Christ.

2 CORINTHIANS 5:21

WANNA READ MORE?

Matthew 26:47-75; 27:1-31
Mark 14:43-72; 15:1-20
Luke 22:47-71; 23:1-25
John 18:1-40; 19:1-16

The soldiers mocked Jesus and rammed a crown of thorns on his head. They yelled and spit at him and beat him. And that's where we'll stop for now. At that exact, horrible place.

Remember, Jesus was innocent. He'd done nothing wrong. Not a thing. Not ever. Yet he was condemned to die anyway. It wasn't fair. But that's how it went down.

See you soon, friends.

47.
JESUS TRULY DIED

Zuri-Claire has this really solemn look on her face, like she isn't thinking about writing me a note at all. I know how she feels. It's like . . . when we're going through all this huge stuff about Jesus, we can't even think about notes for a while.

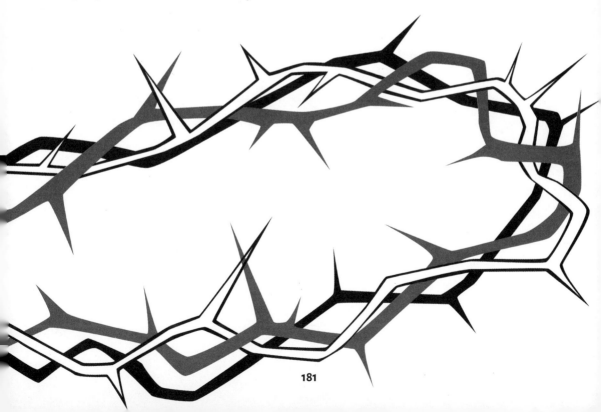

Ahem.

Well, they led Jesus away to be crucified. This is a strange part of Jesus' story. It's very sad. Yet it's also very happy—in a big-picture sort of way—which I'll explain soon. But things will get worse before they get better.

Jesus had been up all night without any sleep, and he'd been whipped and punched and kicked and whipped again. The Roman soldiers forced Jesus to carry a heavy wooden cross—and Jesus was pretty beat up by then, so the soldiers grabbed a guy from the crowd named Simon and made him carry it instead. Jesus' destination was a hillside called Golgotha, which means "Place of the Skull" in the Aramaic language. Some people know the place by its Latin name, Calvary.

When they got to Golgotha, Roman soldiers nailed Jesus to the cross by driving heavy spikes through his hands and feet. Then the soldiers gambled for his clothes. He had a nice, expensive robe, so they didn't tear it apart, but threw dice to see who'd get to keep it. They didn't know it, but the soldiers' silly game fulfilled prophecy.

A sign was fastened above Jesus' head that read, "This is Jesus, the King of the Jews." Pilate had written it, and some uptight dudes tried to get Pilate to change it to "Jesus SAID, I am the King of the Jews," but Pilate wouldn't have any editing. "Not gonna change it," Pilate said. "What I have written, I have written."

It was about nine in the morning on that Friday, which has strangely come to be known as Good Friday. Two thieves were crucified along with Jesus, one on his right, the other on his left. Passersby yelled insults: "Look at you now! If you're really the Son of God, then save yourself and come down from the cross!"

One of the thieves said with a sneer, "So you're the Savior of the world, huh? Prove it! How about saving yourself—and us, too, while you're at it."

But the other thief said, "No. We deserve to die for our crimes. But this man hasn't done anything wrong." Then he spoke to Jesus directly: "Jesus, remember me when you come into your Kingdom."

And Jesus replied, "I promise, today you will be with me in Paradise."

He didn't have strength to talk much while hanging on the cross, but one wonderful thing Jesus said was, "Father, forgive them, for they don't know what they're doing."

Standing near the cross were Jesus' mother and a few of Jesus' followers. (His adoptive dad, Joseph, had probably died earlier.) Jesus' mom stood next to John, and Jesus told her, "From now on, John will look after you."

Jesus hung on the cross in great pain as the hours ticked away. Ten o'clock. Eleven. Noon. Darkness fell across the whole land. The light from the sun could not be seen. One o'clock. Two. Three.

Jesus called in a loud voice, "My God, my God, why have you abandoned me?!"

Time kept ticking. Jesus said, "I'm thirsty." A sponge was soaked in sour wine and held to his lips so he could sip from it.

Then Jesus shouted out one final time and released his spirit, calling, "Father, I trust my spirit into your hands. IT IS FINISHED!"

Jesus bowed his head.

And Jesus died.

What actually happened there on the cross? Was it simply that Jesus died instead of us dying? Yes, but it was much more. Grandpa McCook explained to me that Jesus actually took the punishment on the cross for sin so that we wouldn't need to. Jesus, who had never sinned, became the offering for our sin, so that we could be made right with God. Jesus became our Passover Lamb. When Jesus said, "It is finished," he meant that the payment for our sin was fully paid!

Remember one thing: Jesus truly died.

Take care, kiddos. See you soon.

KIRBY'S NOTES

STICK INSIDE YOUR BRAIN

He was pierced for our rebellion, crushed for our sins. He was beaten so we could be whole. He was whipped so we could be healed. All of us, like sheep, have strayed away. We have left God's paths to follow our own. Yet the LORD laid on him the sins of us all.

ISAIAH 53:5-6

WANNA READ MORE?

Matthew 27:32-50
Mark 15:21-37
Luke 23:26-46
John 19:17-30

48.
JESUS IS BURIED

Zuri-Claire kind of walked close to me as she came into class this morning, and said, "This Jesus story, it really is awesome, huh?" My voice didn't seem to work, but I nodded yes.

Ahem. Hi, guys.

We'll continue with our awesome story of Jesus today. Remember, we just passed the very worst moment in all of history—the moment God the Son died—which turned out to be the very best moment in all of history.

At that very moment when Jesus died, the thick, heavy curtain in the sanctuary of the Temple was mysteriously torn in two, from top to bottom. Grandpa McCook told me the ripping showed that the way for people to come into God's presence was now opened up by Jesus' death.

Even the earth itself couldn't seem to hold back the excitement. The ground shook in a massive earthquake. Rocks split apart. And in the moments and hours just after Jesus died, some strange and amazing things happened to other people.

One of the most amazing was this: in Jerusalem, tombs opened right up, and the bodies of many godly men and women who'd died were raised from the dead. These folks walked around the city saying hello to old friends. Plenty of other people saw them and must have done a double take. But the raised people were really alive.

A Roman officer, kind of a bigwig who had charge over 100 soldiers, stood near the cross along with other soldiers. They were all terrified of the earthquake. This officer, called a centurion, said, "Truly, this man was the Son of God." Some of the others murmured and nodded along with him, so some of Jesus' worst enemies did a switcheroo right there at the foot of the cross and started believing in him.

The uptight religious leaders talked among themselves and decided they didn't want the bodies hanging on the crosses any longer, because of the Passover holiday coming up, so they asked Pilate to hurry along the three deaths by ordering the men's legs to be broken. (That would make it lots harder for a person to push upward so they could breathe, and they would suffocate to death pretty quickly.) But when the soldiers came to Jesus, they saw he was already dead. So they didn't break his legs. One of the soldiers took his spear and pierced Jesus' side, and blood and water flowed out, another sign of death. And that fulfilled another prophecy.

Some of the women who followed Jesus were still there. They'd been watching the crucifixion from a little distance. They seemed to be hanging around afterward to try to see what would be done with Jesus' body.

Late Friday afternoon, a secret disciple of Jesus named Joseph of Arimathea, along with Nicodemus (the man who'd come to see Jesus at night), asked Pilate for permission to take down Jesus' body. Pilate agreed, so the two men wrapped about 75 pounds of perfumed ointment and long strips of cloth around Jesus' body, as was the custom for burial in those days, and laid him in a tomb, which was a cave carved into a rocky cliff. The tomb belonged to Joseph, and it had never been used before. And they rolled a huge, heavy stone across the entrance.

Some of the grumpy religious leaders asked Pilate to seal the tomb, and he also posted armed guards around it. There was no way, nohow, Jesus' body was going anywhere.

The women saw where the body was laid and went home to prepare spices and perfumes, which they were going to put on Jesus' body, according to the customs of the day. But they waited through Saturday because they rested on the Sabbath day as God had told them to do. They must have all been pretty discouraged as the hours of Saturday ticked by. It seemed like all they had hoped for was smashed, and besides that, they'd lost their best friend.

Okay, that's all been some sad stuff, I know. But I mentioned this story has a happy part to it too. We'll see that part next.

KIRBY'S NOTES

STICK INSIDE YOUR BRAIN

I passed on to you what was most important and what had also been passed on to me. Christ died for our sins, just as the Scriptures said. He was buried, and he was raised from the dead on the third day, just as the Scriptures said.

1 CORINTHIANS 15:3-4

WANNA READ MORE?

Matthew 27:51-61

Mark 15:38-47

Luke 23:47-56

John 19:31-42

49.
JESUS TRULY LIVES

Well, Zuri-Claire just sent me a note. It said,

And then she wrote her name and five smiley faces beside it. FIVE! SMILEY! FACES!!!!

I wrote a note in return and sent it right back. The note said,

> You and I are really good
> friends, Kirby.
> Have a GREAT day.
>
> -Zuri-Claire
> ☺ ☺ ☺ ☺ ☺

> You know, I think I
> like that. I like it a lot.
>
> -Kirby
> ♈ ♈ ♈ ♈ ♈

With my name and five smiley faces of my own.

Zuri-Claire read the note just now and she looked up and gave me a grin.

And I gave her a grin right back.

Friends. Yeah. That's what we'll be.

(Sigh.)

Hoo boy, what a relief. When you're 12, being friends is so much stinking better than dating!!!

Ahem.

Early Sunday morning, as the new day was dawning, two women both named Mary and their friend Salome went to visit the tomb. They'd purchased burial spices, and they wanted to put them on Jesus' body. On the way, they asked each other, "Hey, how are we going to roll that stone away?"

But when they got to the tomb, the stone was pushed aside. They walked inside the tomb and saw a young man there, clothed in a white robe. His face shone like lightning, and his clothes were as brilliantly white as snow on a sunshiny day.

The women were all like, "Wha-wha-what?!"

The young man (actually an angel) said, "Don't be scared. You're looking for Jesus, who was crucified. He isn't here! He's risen from the dead!"

Mary Magdalene ran and found Peter the Rock and John the Son of Thunder, and they all ran to the tomb. John ran faster than Peter and got there first and saw the empty graveclothes. Peter got there and saw the same thing. Eventually they left, but Mary still stood outside the tomb, crying. She couldn't take in all that was happening. As she turned to leave, someone standing nearby asked, "Dear woman, why are you crying?"

At first, Mary thought he was the gardener. She said, "Sir, if you've taken him away, tell me where you've put him, and I'll go get him."

The "gardener" just said one word: "Mary!"

She recognized him then and exclaimed, "Teacher!"

"Don't hug me just yet," Jesus said. "Go find my brothers and tell them I'm soon ascending to God my Father and your Father too."

She ran to find the disciples and told them, "I've seen the Lord!"

Some soldiers who'd guarded the tomb went into the city and told the uppity leaders that the body was gone. Mighty worried, they called a meeting and decided to tell people that Jesus' disciples had stolen the body. Then they paid the soldiers to keep their mouths shut.

That same day, two of Jesus' followers were walking to the village of Emmaus, seven miles from Jerusalem. As they walked, they talked about everything that had happened. Suddenly they noticed another man walking with them. (It was Jesus, but God prevented them from recognizing him at first.)

The man asked, "What are you guys talking about?"

Both followers were really sad. One said, "You must be the only person in Jerusalem who doesn't know what's going on."

"Humor me," Jesus said.

So they told him.

Jesus said, "All these things that have happened were predicted by the prophets." And Jesus started from the beginning of Scripture and took them through the writings of Moses and all the prophets, explaining things about himself.

As they neared Emmaus, the two disciples asked Jesus to stay with them. So they went in for supper. Jesus blessed the food, and suddenly their eyes were opened and they recognized him. JESUS!

At that very moment, he disappeared.

The two disciples raced back to Jerusalem to tell the others. It was Sunday evening, and the other disciples were meeting in a locked room because they were afraid. Maybe they'd be arrested next! Suddenly Jesus stood there with them. "Don't worry," he said. "It's me." He showed them the wounds in his hands

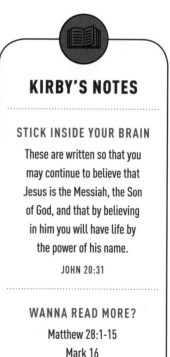

KIRBY'S NOTES

STICK INSIDE YOUR BRAIN
These are written so that you may continue to believe that Jesus is the Messiah, the Son of God, and that by believing in him you will have life by the power of his name.

JOHN 20:31

WANNA READ MORE?
Matthew 28:1-15
Mark 16
Luke 24:1-49
John 20:1-20

and side, and they were all filled with joy. Jesus asked, "Do you have anything here to eat?"

They gave him a piece of broiled fish, and he ate it. Then he said, "Peace be with you. The Father has sent me, and now I'm sending you." He added, "Stay here in the city until the Holy Spirit comes and fills you with power from heaven."

Wow. What will happen next? We'll find out next week.

50.
JESUS HEADS FOR HOME

Noah came into the classroom today rubbing his hands, saying, "Okay, Kirby McCook, what happens next? Give us another bucket of that awesome sauce!"

"You got it!" I answered, and opened my Bible.

Ahem.

Thomas wasn't there when Jesus walked into that locked room and ten jaws dropped. Later, the other disciples told him, "Jesus is alive." But Thomas said, "Nope. I won't believe it. Not unless I see for myself." So forever after, he was known as "Doubting Thomas," which must have looked silly on the back of his football jersey.

Eight days later, the disciples

The nickname might be a bit harsh.

were together again, including Doubting Thomas. The door was still locked, and suddenly, just like before, Jesus stood among them. "Peace be with you," he said. Then he looked at Thomas and added, "Look at my hands. Go ahead—touch the wound in my side. Believe."

Thomas said, "My Lord and my God!" and probably fell on his knees in front of Jesus.

Jesus said, "Thomas, you believe because you've seen me. But it's also really good for people to believe without seeing me."

The disciples didn't really know what to do after that, so they went back to fishing in the Sea of Galilee. They took their boat out and fished all night. They fished and fished and fished, but they didn't catch anything. At sunrise, Jesus stood on the beach, but the disciples couldn't see who it was. Jesus called, "Friends, how's that working out for you? Did you catch anything?"

"Um, nope," they said. "But you should have seen the one that got away."

"Try throwing your net on the right-hand side of the boat," Jesus called from shore.

Now, these guys were experienced fishermen. They'd tried everything they could think of. You can almost hear their mutterings. *Oh, the right side. Of course! We didn't think of that, did we?* But they threw their net on the right anyway. Immediately the fish started showing up like crazy. So many fish jumped into their nets that they couldn't haul them into the boat.

John said, "It's Jesus." And the message was clear: Jesus knew where the fish were. Jesus knew how life worked. Jesus knew what his followers should do—not just how to fish, but how to live.

That's when Peter got a clue. He jumped into the water and swam for shore while the others wrestled the nets and brought the boat and fish to land. They counted 153 big ones.

When they got ashore, the disciples found a cheery bonfire waiting and Jesus barbecuing fish and making toast. "Come and have breakfast!" he said, grinning at their stunned faces.

This was all good, but one guy still needed a special face-to-face with Jesus—Peter the Rock, who'd denied Christ three times. After breakfast, Jesus asked Peter, "Do you love me more than these?" He might have been talking about the other disciples, or maybe the fish. Either way, it's cool what Jesus DIDN'T SAY to Peter. Jesus DIDN'T SAY, "You're lame. You denied me. THREE TIMES. What were you thinking, doofus?!" Nope. No scolding. That's pretty cool grace right there.

"Sure, Jesus," Peter said. "I love you. You know that."

They talked some more, and all was forgiven.

Altogether, after Jesus came back to life from being full-on dead, he was seen by more than five hundred people.

Later, the eleven remaining disciples met up with Jesus on a mountain. They hung on his every word, maybe because they had a hunch that these were the last words Jesus would speak during his first coming on this earth:

> I've been given all authority in heaven and on earth. So, go and tell people in every country on the earth about me and my Good News so they can be my disciples too. Baptize people in the name of the Father, the Son, and the Holy Spirit. Teach these new disciples to obey all the commands I've given you. And be sure of this: I'm with you always, even to the end of time.

When Jesus had finished talking with them, he just went up, straight into heaven. There, he sat

KIRBY'S NOTES

STICK INSIDE YOUR BRAIN
Go and make disciples of all the nations, baptizing them in the name of the Father and the Son and the Holy Spirit. Teach these new disciples to obey all the commands I have given you. And be sure of this: I am with you always, even to the end of the age.

MATTHEW 28:19-20

WANNA READ MORE?
Matthew 28:16-20
Luke 24:50-52
John 20:24–21:25
Acts 1:7-11

down in the place of honor at God the Father's right hand. The disciples stared into the clouds, probably with their mouths hanging open. Then two white-robed men suddenly appeared and said, "Don't just stand here staring. Jesus went to heaven. He'll return someday just this same way."

"Oh," the disciples said. "Okay." And they headed back to Jerusalem, taking the first steps to obey Jesus' last instructions.

You might think that's the end of Jesus' story, but it's not, as we'll soon see.

Remember, Jesus truly died and then truly came alive, and he keeps on living today.

See ya later, all you silly alligators.

51.

JESUS' STORY CONTINUES FOREVER AND EVER AND EVER AND EVER

Well, TONS has happened since last week. My mom was at the grocery store on Tuesday getting lasagna and stuff, and guess who she ran into! Yep—Mrs. Higgins, our old teacher! She asked, "Did you ever find anybody to teach junior church? I feel so sorry for bailing on the class like I did, but I just couldn't take any more of that boy Jimmy and his gargantuan sneezes."

And Mom said, "I have absolutely no idea what you're talking about."

So later that evening, after supper, Mom asked me, "Kirby, who's been teaching junior church lately?"

Dad walked into the room right then, and I had that feeling like I'd been making a surprise Christmas gift for my parents all year, but they found out what it was before it was wrapped and under the tree. Then the whole story came out. Both of my parents' jaws hung open, and they were like, "You've been teaching junior church

People tell me I have her eyes.

this whole year!?!?" Dad was like, "I wondered why you were hanging out at Grandpa McCook's apartment so much."

They started texting other parents like crazy, and I guess we kids all explained how the only reason we kept it a secret for so long was that we were afraid of getting boring Mr. Cowburn to be our substitute again, and you know the rest of the story. Apparently, Grandpa McCook's phone was ringing off the hook, but after a while he conveniently got laryngitis and couldn't talk. I'm pretty sure his eyes were twinkling. The children's minister, Mr. Javier, called a meeting of the parents and explained all about our big, fun experiment and how he checked up on me and Grandpa McCook regularly, and I guess there was quite a bit of talk about "kids-taking-responsibility" and "knowing-more-than-we-thought" and "got-to-give-them-credit" and "well-how-about-that!"

So guess who's now got two thumbs and a permanent job teaching junior church?!

Yep, this guy.

Ahem.

All right, everybody, the story of Jesus wouldn't be complete without talking about one more guy. His name was Saul, and nope, he wasn't the lousy king of Israel named Saul. This Saul, a different Saul, lived in the first century AD, and he hated anybody and everybody who followed Jesus.

How bad was this Saul? Well, he went from house to house searching for followers of Jesus, and when he found them, he dragged them out into the street and threw them in jail. Imagine if you and your family got hauled out of your beds one night and tossed into jail just because you follow Jesus! A righteous dude named Stephen was even killed because he followed Jesus, and Saul was in hearty agreement with putting him to death. Saul helpfully held the coats of the murderers who picked up stones and threw them at Stephen till he died.

But everything changed one day when Saul took a trip to the city of Damascus. His purpose? To arrest followers of Jesus and bring them back to Jerusalem in chains.

That's where Jesus enters the story.

Yes, Jimmy? You thought he went back to heaven? Well, he did, but he's not limited. He can go anywhere he wants.

As Saul was traveling along, a bright light shone on him like a spotlight. He fell to the ground, and a voice from heaven called, "Saul! Saul! Why are you persecuting me?"

"Who are you?" Saul asked.

The voice replied, "I'm Jesus, the one you're persecuting. Now get up and go into the city, and you'll be told what to do."

Saul was blind when he got up, but his companions led him to Damascus. To make a long story short, after meeting Jesus that day, Saul decided that Jesus was totally worth following. Saul regained his vision, and he spent the rest of his life traveling around telling people about Jesus. He's known by his Gentile name, Paul, in most of the New Testament, because Jesus gave him the mission of telling the Good News to the non-Jewish people of the Roman Empire. Through the inspiration of the Holy Spirit, Paul eventually wrote a big chunk of the New Testament, and after his Damascus Road experience, pretty much all Paul ever wanted to do was live for Jesus.

I guess it's kind of been like that ever since for anybody who meets Jesus. Once you know who he truly is, you want to follow him everywhere!

We'll wrap this up next week. After a while, crocodiles.

KIRBY'S NOTES

STICK INSIDE YOUR BRAIN

I want to know Christ and experience the mighty power that raised him from the dead. I want to suffer with him, sharing in his death, so that one way or another I will experience the resurrection from the dead!

PHILIPPIANS 3:10-11

WANNA READ MORE?

Acts 8:1-3; 9:1-31

Galatians 1:11-17

Philippians 3:6-10

52.
JESUS WINS

A bunch of us hung around after class to plan a year-end party—I voted for another skating party (you know why), but most kids wanted a beach bash, and majority wins. (Anybody know where I can get a crash course in how to swim?)

Zuri-Claire was one of the party planners, and here's a funny thing: now that I know we're friends, I can talk to her just like any other human being. I even told a lame joke, and she laughed and said, "Good one, Kirbs."

Did you know, she has this really cute dimple in her chin? (If you tell anybody I said that, I'll punch your lights out!)

Ahem. Let's get started, you bright-eyed bunch.

If you thought the story of Jesus was over, think again. His story doesn't end with Paul and not even with the last page of the Bible. Jesus Christ is alive today, and his main job is to be the head of the church—that's his bunch of followers. Jesus still saves people today, and we can talk to Jesus whenever. That's called prayer. Through Jesus we can do all the things he wants us to do, because he supplies the strength. He's described as the author of our faith, and he writes our life story along with us, continually working to shape us into the image of God.

The story of Jesus doesn't end with the likes of us, either. When the apostle John, one of the Sons of Thunder, became an old man, he was exiled to the island of Patmos. That means he was sent off to live alone because the religious leaders thought he was a troublemaker and didn't know what to do with his teachings about Jesus. There on Patmos, under the Holy Spirit's guidance, John wrote a book called Revelation about the future of people and the world and pretty much everything.

Jesus shows up in Revelation quite a bit. I asked Grandpa McCook to explain the book of Revelation, and he said basically things get worse before they get better, and then in the end Jesus wins. One of the best things that John talks about in Revelation is that Jesus is coming to earth again someday!

When he does, he'll come from heaven with a commanding shout and a loud trumpet sound. First, believers who've died will rise from their graves. Then, together with them, those of us who are still alive and remain on earth will be caught up in the clouds to meet the Lord in the air.

In Revelation, Jesus is called the First and the Last. He's also called Faithful and True. Jesus is a warrior King at the end of time, and the armies of heaven follow him on white horses. From the mouth of Jesus comes a sharp sword to strike down all remaining evil, which is probably picture language to tell us that Jesus defeats enemies with his words. On Jesus' robe is written the title King of all kings and Lord of all lords, and at the name of Jesus, every knee will bow.

At the end of time, everything is set right. Jesus makes a new heaven and earth for us. Adam and Eve's curse no longer applies to the world, and everything is made new again. God lives with his people, and there won't be any more crying or death or sorrow or pain. We'll live in a supercool, multidimensional city where we won't even need a sun or moon, because the glory of God will light up everything. It's going to be a really, really good time. And Jesus the Savior will be Jesus the King of Everything.

What are we supposed to do in the meantime? We're not supposed to argue about what's going to happen in the end. Or worry about things. Or try and figure out exactly when it's going to happen. We're supposed to EN-COURAGE ONE ANOTHER with these words:

Jesus is coming back again someday!

So there you have it. Are you encouraging your friends with those words?

Hey, our look into Jesus—who he is and what he does—is over for Kirby and his class for now. But the Story of Jesus is never finished. He's always with us Jesus kids. See you all next week. It's lunchtime, I'm HUNGRY, and I'm going to go get a cheeseburger.

KIRBY'S NOTES

STICK INSIDE YOUR BRAIN

The Lord himself will come down from heaven with a commanding shout, with the voice of the archangel, and with the trumpet call of God. First, the believers who have died will rise from their graves. Then, together with them, we who are still alive and remain on the earth will be caught up in the clouds to meet the Lord in the air. Then we will be with the Lord forever. So encourage each other with these words.

1 THESSALONIANS 4:16-18

WANNA READ MORE?

Philippians 2:10
1 Thessalonians 4:13-18
1 Corinthians 15:51-53
Revelation 19:11-16; 22:13

ABOUT THE AUTHORS

 **STEVE ARTERBURN** used to be a fifth-grade teacher, so he likes kids just fine. These days, he's a family counselor, the founder and chairman of New Life Ministries, and the host of the number one nationally syndicated Christian counseling talk show *New Life Live!* heard and watched by more than two million people each week.

A *New York Times* bestselling author, Steve is the developer and editor of ten different specialty and study Bibles, three of which were nominated for Bible of the Year and one which won the award.

Steve's books include *Every Man's Battle*, *Toxic Faith*, *Lose It for Life*, *Healing Is a Choice*, *The Life Recovery Bible*, *Every Man's Bible*, and *Spiritual Renewal Bible*. He has received three Platinum Book Awards for writing and publishing excellence.

Steve has degrees from Baylor University (elementary education) and University of North Texas (counseling) as well as two honorary doctorate degrees. He serves as one of the teaching pastors at Heartland Church in Indianapolis, where he lives with his wife and family.

M. N. BROTHERTON is the *New York Times* bestselling author or coauthor of more than 25 books.

A Christy Award winner for writing excellence, he has a bachelor's degree in biblical education and journalism from Multnomah University and a master's degree in practical theology and writing from Talbot School of Theology at Biola University.

He and his wife have three children and live in Bellingham, Washington, where they enjoy bike riding and eating ice cream.

FOR ADVENTURERS

The Wormling series

The Dopple Ganger Chronicles

FOR COMEDIANS

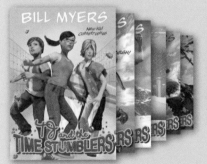

TJ and the Time Stumblers series

Be Your Own Duck Commander series

FOR ANIMAL LOVERS

Winnie the Horse Gentler series

Starlight Animal Rescue series

DIVE DEEPER

into God's Word with these

DEVOTIONALS FOR TEENS!